Compiled and Arranged by Jim Beloff

SONGS

Edited by Ronny S. Schiff
Cover and Art Direction by Elizabeth Maihock Beloff
Graphics and Music Typography by Charylu Roberts

Foreword

Thanks to the current wave of ukulele popularity, there has been a growing interest in the largest member of the family, the baritone ukulele. Fifty percent larger than the better-known soprano size, the baritone offers the player the ease-of-play of the ukulele with the deeper tones of a nylon-string guitar (minus its two lowest strings.) And, like all ukuleles, it's fun to play as a solo instrument or to accompany singing.

The baritone was introduced to the world in the 1950s, thanks mostly to media superstar Arthur Godfrey who played one on his many TV and radio shows. Godfrey had a nice jazzy way with the instrument that complemented his mellow baritone voice. A Godfrey standard, "Makin' Love Ukulele Style," is included here.

For this collection we decided to take some of our favorite songs from our other *Jumpin' Jim's* books and arrange them especially for the baritone. It turned out to be a revelation on two levels. The first is that the warmth of the bari seemed to favor ballads and swing rhythms. The other discovery was how much the low D string (instead of the traditional "my dog has fleas" string relationship) changed the quality of the basic chords. If nothing else, it reminded us of how nice it is to have a few different-sized ukes around the house.

In his method book, *The Baritone Ukulele*, published in 1951, Herk Favilla admits that "the baritone was primarily developed with the thought in mind to simplify guitar study for the beginner, since it has the same tuning as the first four strings of the guitar." While it can still serve as a bridge to the six string guitar, the baritone uke has its own unique musical charms. Play through any of the songs in this book and discover for yourself the beauty of the bari!

Thanks "bari" much to Liz Beloff, Tom Favilla, Gruhn Guitars, John King, Charylu Roberts, Dan Sawyer, Ronny Schiff and Pete "Uncle Zac" Zaccagnino for their help with this project.

—Jumpin' Jim Beloff

How To Use This Book

There are four different sizes in the ukulele family. From small to large they are: soprano, concert, tenor and baritone. The three smaller sizes are most often tuned GCEA (or in some cases a whole step higher to ADF♯B). When the strings are played open (with no fingers on the fretboard) they produce that famous "my dog has fleas" melody most people associate with the ukulele.

The baritone ukulele was meant to be tuned a fourth down from GCEA to DGBE and always with a low D, exactly like the four highest strings of a guitar. As a result, the bari lacks the "my dog has fleas" string relationship and most resembles a nylon-string guitar in tone. Nonetheless, the bari has its own unique voice and, because of its four strings, shares the ease of play of the other members of the uke family.

The Family of Ukuleles

Soprano	Concert	Tenor	Baritone
21"	25"	26 1/4"	31"

Like all Jumpin' Jim's ukulele songbooks, this book features chord grids with dots that indicate where you should put your fingers. For beginners, we recommend *Jumpin' Jim's Ukulele Tips 'N' Tunes* or *The Joy Of Uke* #1 DVD to introduce you to the basics of playing the ukulele. Once you've mastered the fundamentals, going between GCEA and DGBE tuning is a snap. All you need to keep in mind is that the names of the chord shapes change. For example, the C chord shape in GCEA is a G chord on a bari. The G7 in GCEA is a D7 on a bari, and so on. We've included a baritone chord chart here that will help to keep all of this straight.

One last point is that if you ignore the chord names here and play the fingerings on a GCEA uke it will sound perfectly fine. The only difference is that the song will sound a fourth higher than written. This works the other way as well. Any songbook arranged for GCEA ukes can be played with a baritone uke, but the song will sound a fourth lower than written. This can be handy if any arrangement is too low or too high to comfortably sing. Have fun!

Baritone Tuning

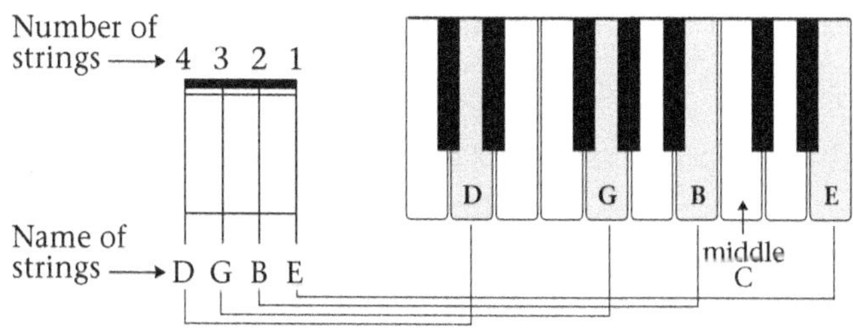

The Favilla Baritone Ukulele

By Tom Favilla

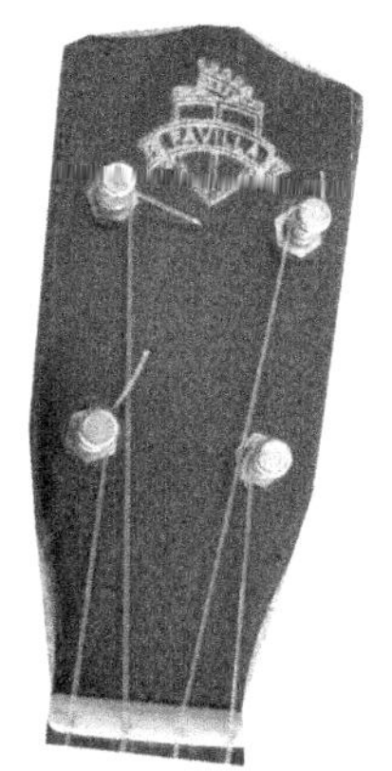

Brothers John and Joseph Favilla first started building musical instruments in 1890, and by 1894 had formed a company called "Favilla Brothers." They produced soprano ukuleles in the late 1890s and early 1900s under the Marca Aquila label. These ukes were distinctive, in that the fingerboard ended at the body and did not extend onto the top of the instrument.

Starting right after WWII, John Favilla built the first baritone ukuleles for his son, Herk Favilla. Herk used them with his very young students and women who couldn't handle a full size guitar. By 1949, the baritone was a regular part of the Favilla line.

Arthur Godfrey, who was already playing Favilla soprano ukes, was introduced to the baritone ukulele by Frank Favilla (Herk's brother), and helped spur its popularity in the early 1950s. There are a few stories, all in error, that other builders with Arthur Godfrey developed the baritone uke, but the simple truth is that Favilla was building them years earlier.

The first baritone method book was written by Herk Favilla in 1949. Godfrey used Favilla instruments for years until he demanded money to continue using them and had a falling out with Frank Favilla. He then thought he made a cunning switch to a "Vinci" ukulele, not realizing that Tomasso Vinciguerra (Vinci) worked for Frank and had given him a Favilla baritone without the Favilla name stamped on it. This inside joke flew for about a year before Godfrey caught on. By then, Vinciguerra had left Favilla to strike out on his own before establishing his string company. (Also about that time, Godfrey switched to the Vega baritone ukulele).

Favilla baritone ukuleles were built until 1985. There were three variations: 1) If there was no label inside the soundhole, then it was built before 1962. 2) A baritone uke with the Favilla name in script (no crest) was built by Herk Favilla between late 1958 and early 1959. These were built in Brooklyn, NY during a 6-month period just before Herk received final control of the family business. Only about 250 to 300 of these were built. In June 1959, Herk took over the family operation in New York City and closed the Brooklyn shop. From that point on, only the familiar crest trademark (first introduced in the 1920s) would ever be used. 3) The third and rarest variation occurred around 1963 when Herk and Thomas Favilla built twelve baritones with spruce tops. Herk wanted a distinctive one for his wife, so he picked out one of the twelve for her.

Herk Favilla

A year after that, he did the same with the C-3 half-size guitar (twenty-four of these were built with spruce tops). The C-3, known as the "Dulcette," was an all mahogany body with a rosewood fingerboard. The body was that of a baritone uke reinforced to take the additional stress of six strings. John Favilla also built concert and tenor size ukuleles, between 1920 and 1940. In addition to the original and more notable baritone uke, John's brother, Joseph, also built violins, cellos, and basses. This variety gave rise to the saying, "If it had strings, Favilla built it."

The first early national notoriety of Favilla soprano ukuleles occurred in 1929, when half a dozen of them accompanied the Byrd expedition to Antarctica. One is still in the Favilla family signed by the members of the "Little America" expedition, including Commander Byrd. It was presented to the Favillas by Dick Konter, the expedition's radio operator.

Once they started producing the baritone ukulele on a regular basis they built anywhere from 25 to 50 units a month until 1973. The list price was $65 in 1949 and $100 in 1973. After 1973, baritone uke production was quite sporadic (no more than a couple of dozen were made per year) and it was discontinued in 1985. Soprano ukuleles were discontinued in 1968.

Thomas Hercules Favilla was born 10/6/42 in Brooklyn, New York. After school he started in the family business sweeping floors and greasing machinery under the watchful eye of grandfather, John Favilla. He entered Favilla Guitars full time in 1962 after his father, Herk Favilla, suffered a heart attack. He married Nancy in 1969 and has two musical sons, T.J. and David. Since 1986 he has been active in the construction industry, building low and moderate income housing in New York City.

B A R I

the
completely
new
BOBBY
Henshaw
ukuleles
BARITONE
MODEL B-15

THE
Islander
BARITONE
designed by MACCAFERRI
28¾" long
10" wide
3½" deep
This is the ukulele everyone has been waiting for. The Islander BARITONE is a full-size, professional instrument, like that used by television's biggest star! It has beautiful, deep, penetrating tone and is easy to play. Made of DOW Styron, a special, highly resounding plastic material. Features professional cutaway . . . extended, precision fingerboard . . . metalized frets . . . nylon-wound strings . . . finest patent pegs. Lavish Rosewood grain and Blonde finish.
Complete with pick, key adjuster and polythene bag.
FRENCH AMERICAN REEDS MFG. CO., Inc.
3050 Webster Avenue
New York 67, N. Y.
Printed in U.S.A.

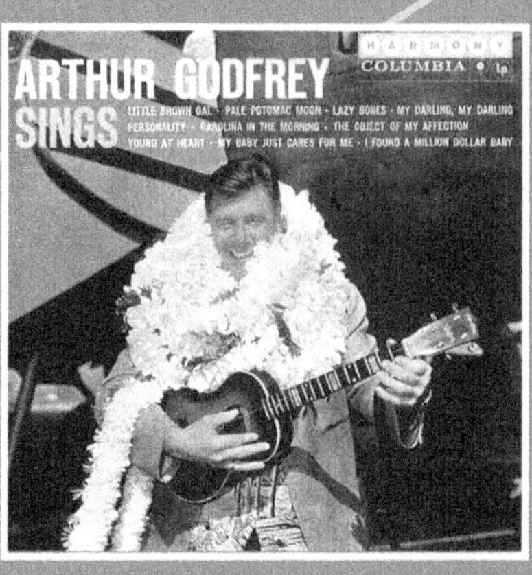

ARTHUR GODFREY
SINGS
HARMONY
COLUMBIA lp
LITTLE BROWN GAL · PALE POTOMAC MOON · LAZY BONES · MY DARLING, MY DARLING
PERSONALITY · CAROLINA IN THE MORNING · THE OBJECT OF MY AFFECTION
YOUNG AT HEART · MY BABY JUST CARES FOR ME · I FOUND A MILLION DOLLAR BABY

ISLANDER®
Baritone
UKE
M M
Designed by
MACCAFERRI
U.S. Pat. No. 2,597,154
U.S. Pat. No. 2,614,448
PATENTS PEND.

HARMONY BARITONE UKULELE

A super size instrument with warmth of tone and ease of response that will delight the exacting player. Is tuned same as first four strings of regular guitar.

No. 695
$42.50

Harmony Baritone Ukulele. Made of seasoned mahogany, nicely figured, well finished. Fingerboard of Brazilian rosewood. Inlaid position markers. Tuning keys are fine quality, strings are carefully gauged nylon. Length of scale 19¼"; width of body 10"; length 13⅞"; length overall 29¾".

No. 695 .... Each **$42.50**

BARITONE UKE

Has BIG CLEAR TONE and GREAT CARRYING POWER!

It's an extra large size: overall length—29½"; large bowl—10"; smaller bowl—7¾"; length of body—12¾"!

ALL THESE FEATURES:—19" scale Rosewood fingerboard, inlaid with 8 pearl position dots on 3rd, 5th, 7th, 10th, 12th and 15th frets . . . 18 frets—14 clear of body . . . inlaid sound-hole . . . mahogany bridge with bone saddle . . . fine patent pegs . . . 2 Nylon strings — 2 strings wound on Nylon!

No. 2744
Each
\$28.95

***"Challenge" Quality* BARITONE UKE CASE**
No. 290
Each
\$6.25

T O N E

Baritone Ukulele Chord Chart

Tune Ukulele

D G B E

MAJOR CHORDS

A | A♯ B♭ | B | C | C♯ D♭ | D | D♯ E♭ | E | F | F♯ G♭ | G | G♯ A♭

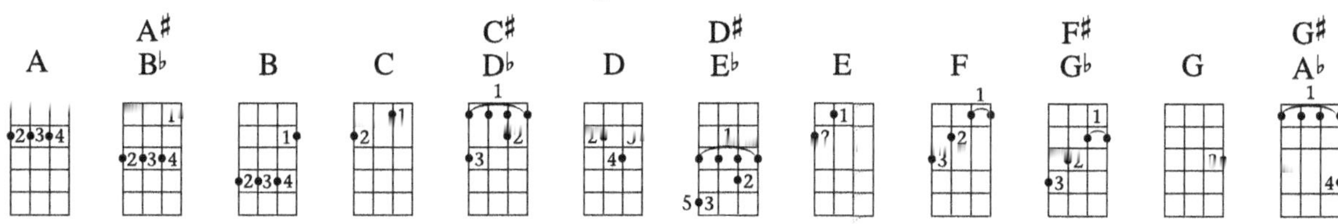

MINOR CHORDS

Am | A♯m B♭m | Bm | Cm | C♯m D♭m | Dm | D♯m E♭m | Em | Fm | F♯m G♭m | Gm | G♯m A♭m

DOMINANT SEVENTH CHORDS

A^7 | $A♯^7$ $B♭^7$ | B^7 | C^7 | $C♯^7$ $D♭^7$ | D^7 | $D♯^7$ $E♭^7$ | E^7 | F^7 | $F♯^7$ $G♭^7$ | G^7 | $G♯^7$ $A♭^7$

DOMINANT NINTH CHORDS

A^9 | $A♯^9$ $B♭^9$ | B^9 | C^9 | $C♯^9$ $D♭^9$ | D^9 | $D♯^9$ $E♭^9$ | E^9 | F^9 | $F♯^9$ $G♭^9$ | G^9 | $G♯^9$ $A♭^9$

MINOR SEVENTH CHORDS

Am^7 | $A♯m^7$ $B♭m^7$ | Bm^7 | Cm^7 | $C♯m^7$ $D♭m^7$ | Dm^7 | $D♯m^7$ $E♭m^7$ | Em^7 | Fm^7 | $F♯m^7$ $G♭m^7$ | Gm^7 | $G♯m^7$ $A♭m^7$

MAJOR SIXTH CHORDS

A^6 | $A♯^6$ $B♭^6$ | B^6 | C^6 | $C♯^6$ $D♭^6$ | D^6 | $D♯^6$ $E♭^6$ | E^6 | F^6 | $F♯^6$ $G♭^6$ | G^6 | $G♯^6$ $A♭^6$

MINOR SIXTH CHORDS

Am^6 · A♯m^6 / B♭m^6 · Bm^6 · Cm^6 · C♯m^6 / D♭m^6 · Dm^6 · D♯m^6 / E♭m^6 · Em^6 · Fm^6 · F♯m^6 / G♭m^6 · Gm^6 · G♯m^6 / A♭m^6

MAJOR SEVENTH CHORDS

Amaj^7 · A♯maj^7 / B♭maj^7 · Bmaj^7 · Cmaj^7 · C♯maj^7 / D♭maj^7 · Dmaj^7 · D♯maj^7 / E♭maj^7 · Emaj^7 · Fmaj^7 · F♯maj^7 / G♭maj^7 · Gmaj^7 · G♯maj^7 / A♭maj^7

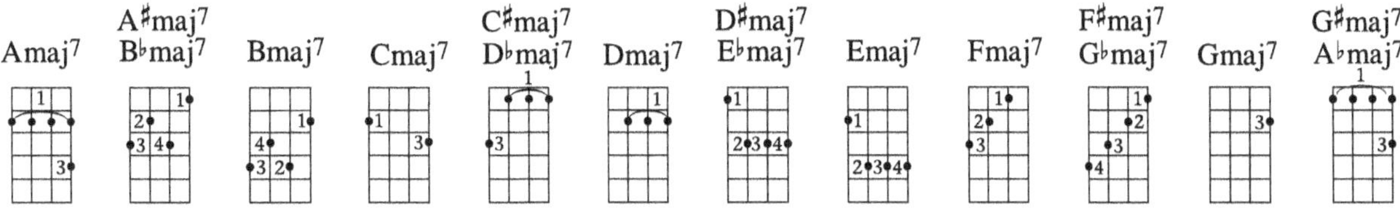

DOMINANT SEVENTH CHORDS WITH RAISED FIFTH (7th+5)

A^{7+5} · A♯$^{7+5}$ / B♭$^{7+5}$ · B^{7+5} · C^{7+5} · C♯$^{7+5}$ / D♭$^{7+5}$ · D^{7+5} · D♯$^{7+5}$ / E♭$^{7+5}$ · E^{7+5} · F^{7+5} · F♯$^{7+5}$ / G♭$^{7+5}$ · G^{7+5} · G♯$^{7+5}$ / A♭$^{7+5}$

DOMINANT SEVENTH CHORDS WITH LOWERED FIFTH (7th♭5)

A$^{7♭5}$ · A♯$^{7♭5}$ / B♭$^{7♭5}$ · B$^{7♭5}$ · C$^{7♭5}$ · C♯$^{7♭5}$ / D♭$^{7♭5}$ · D$^{7♭5}$ · D♯$^{7♭5}$ / E♭$^{7♭5}$ · E$^{7♭5}$ · F$^{7♭5}$ · F♯$^{7♭5}$ / G♭$^{7♭5}$ · G$^{7♭5}$ · G♯$^{7♭5}$ / A♭$^{7♭5}$

AUGMENTED FIFTH CHORDS (aug or +)

Aaug · A♯aug / B♭aug · Baug · Caug · C♯aug / D♭aug · Daug · D♯aug / E♭aug · Eaug · Faug · F♯aug / G♭aug · Gaug · G♯aug / A♭aug

DIMINISHED SEVENTH CHORDS (dim)

Adim · A♯dim / B♭dim · Bdim · Cdim · C♯dim / D♭dim · Ddim · D♯dim / E♭dim · Edim · Fdim · F♯dim / G♭dim · Gdim · G♯dim / A♭dim

Any Time

* ○ Play this string open.
x Means don't play that string.

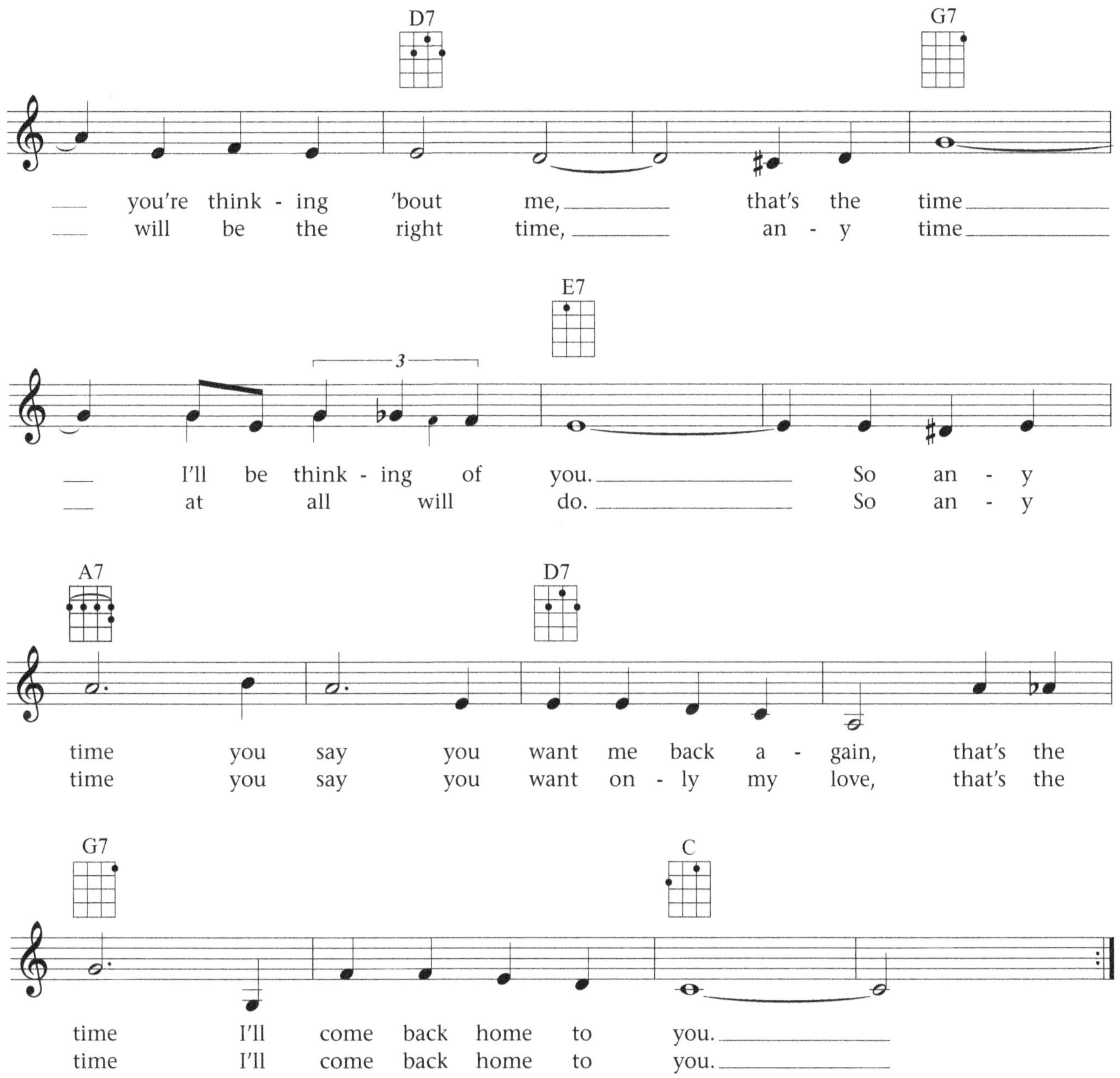

D7 G7

__ you're think - ing 'bout me, ____ that's the time ____
__ will be the right time, ____ an - y time ____

E7

__ I'll be think - ing of you. ____ So an - y
__ at all will do. ____ So an - y

A7 D7

time you say you want me back a - gain, that's the
time you say you want on - ly my love, that's the

G7 C

time I'll come back home to you. ____
time I'll come back home to you. ____

As Time Goes By

Words and Music by
HERMAN HUPFELD

*This is an alternate form of A7.

G G7 C E7
Moon-light and love songs nev - er out of date,
Am C♯dim
hearts full of pas - sion, jeal - ous - y and hate;
Em A7
wom - an needs man and man must have his mate, that
D7 G♯dim D7 Am7 D7
no one can de - ny. It's still the same old sto - ry, a
Dm(add B) D7 G D+ G Bm
fight for love and glo - ry, a case of do or die! The
A7 G Gdim Am7 D7 G F9 G
world will al - ways wel - come lov - ers, as time goes by.

Blue Hawaii

First Note
Words and Music by
LEO ROBIN and RALPH RAINGER
Moderately
A7 Cdim A7 D B7
Per - fume in the air and rare flow - ers ev - 'ry - where, and
Em A7 D A7 Cdim
white shad - ows we could share at Wai - ki - ki.
A sky full of
A7 F♯7 Bm E9 E7
stars and soft far - a - way gui - tars, it seems to be on - ly a
A7 D D7 G D
a tempo
rev - er - ie.
Night and you and blue Ha - wa - ii,
B7 E7 A7 D
the night is heav - en - ly and you are heav - en to me.

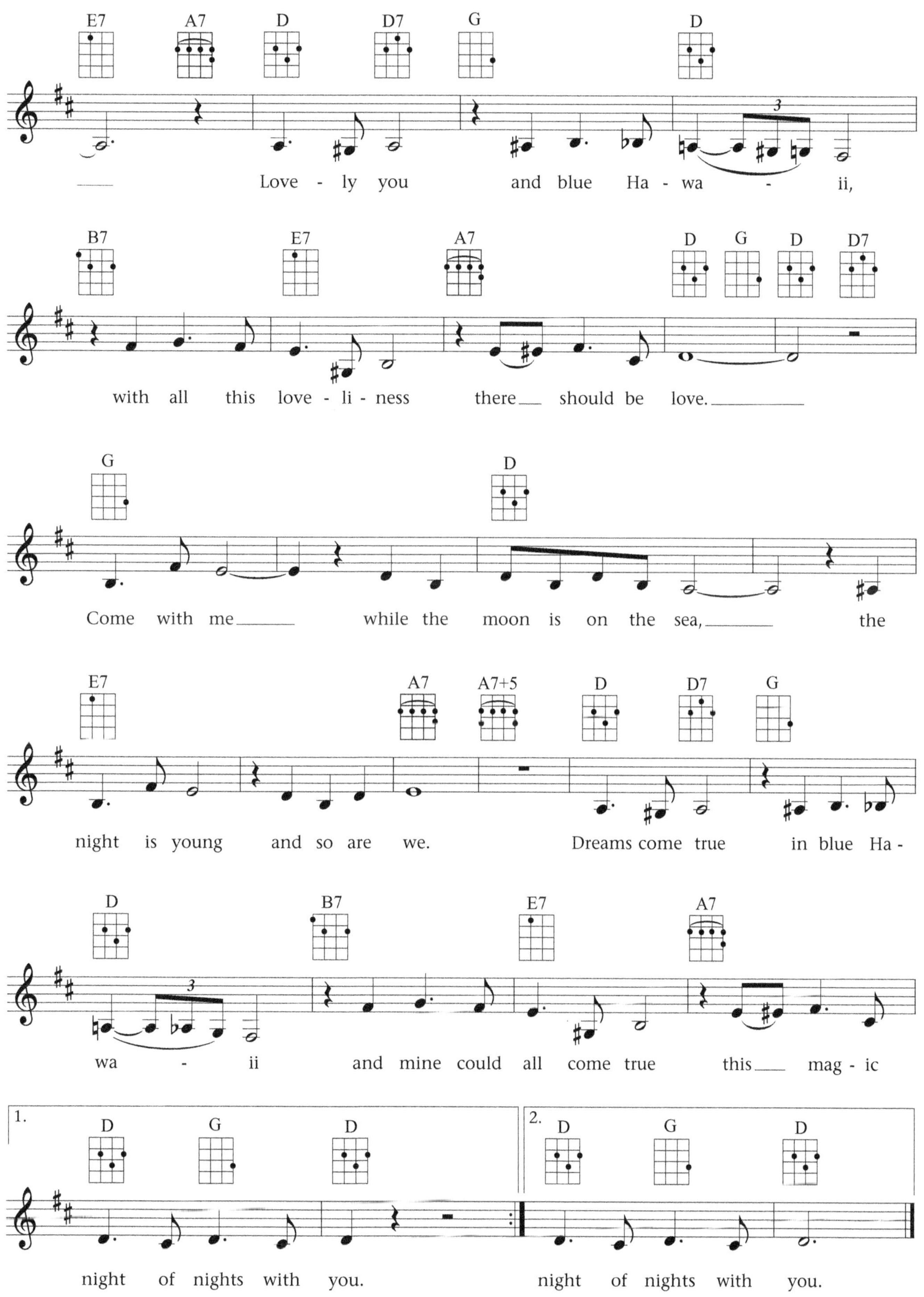
E7
A7
D
D7
G
D
Love - ly you and blue Ha - wa - ii,
B7
E7
A7
D
G
D
D7
with all this love - li - ness there should be love.
G
D
Come with me while the moon is on the sea, the
E7
A7
A7+5
D
D7
G
night is young and so are we. Dreams come true in blue Ha -
D
B7
E7
A7
wa - ii and mine could all come true this mag - ic
1.
D
G
D
night of nights with you.
2.
D
G
D
night of nights with you.

Blue Moon

Words by
LORENZ HART

Music by
RICHARD RODGERS

C Dm7 C Dm7 G7
for. And then there sud - den - ly ap - peared be -
C Dm7 G7 C
fore me the on - ly one my arms will ev - er hold. I heard some -
Fm B♭7 E♭ G D7
bod - y whis - per "Please a - dore me" and when I looked the moon had turned to
Dm7 G7 C Am Dm7 G7
gold! Blue moon, now I'm no long - er a - lone
C Am Dm7 G7 C Am
with - out a dream in my heart,
Dm7 C Dm7 C
with - out a love of my own.

Blue Skies

Words and Music by
IRVING BERLIN

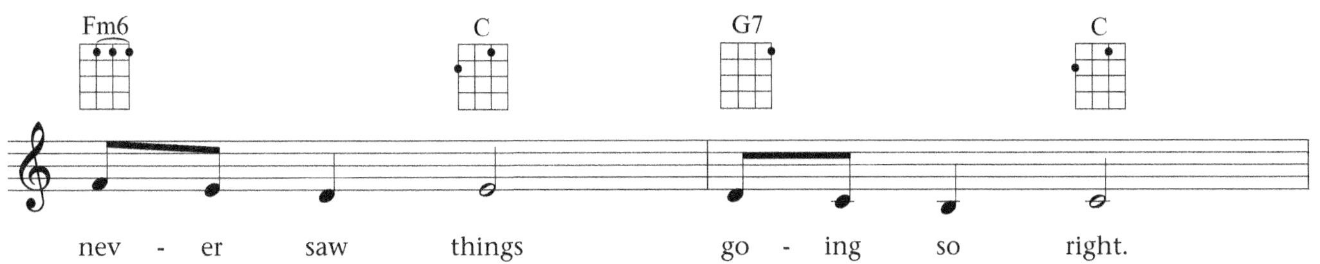
Fm6
C
G7
C
nev - er saw things go - ing so right.

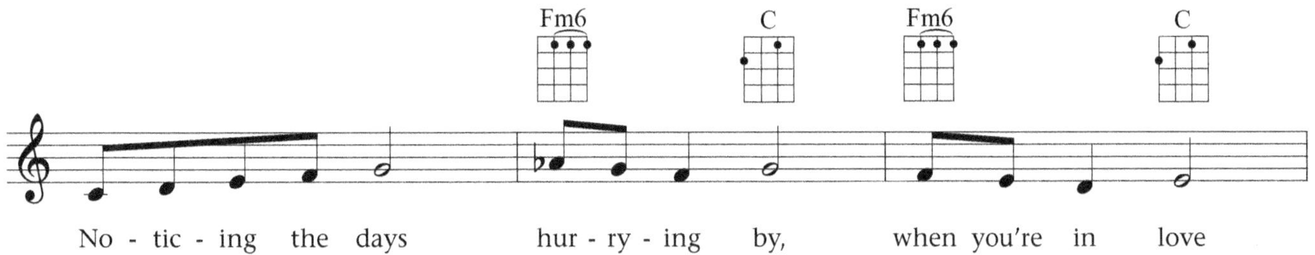
Fm6
C
Fm6
C
No - tic - ing the days hur - ry - ing by, when you're in love

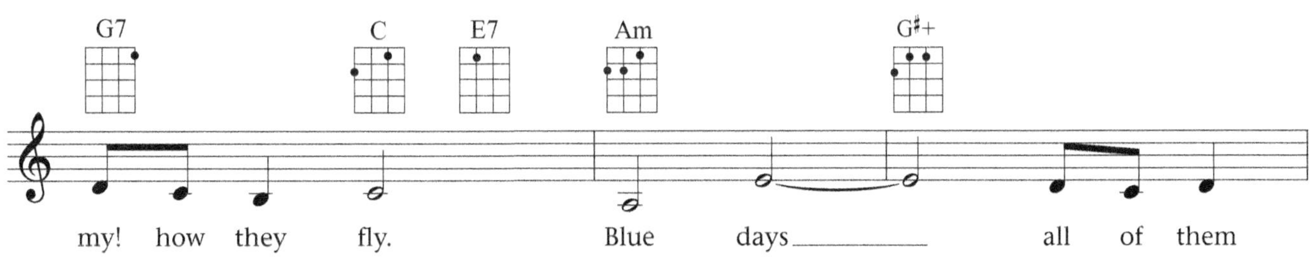
G7
C
E7
Am
G♯+
my! how they fly. Blue days all of them

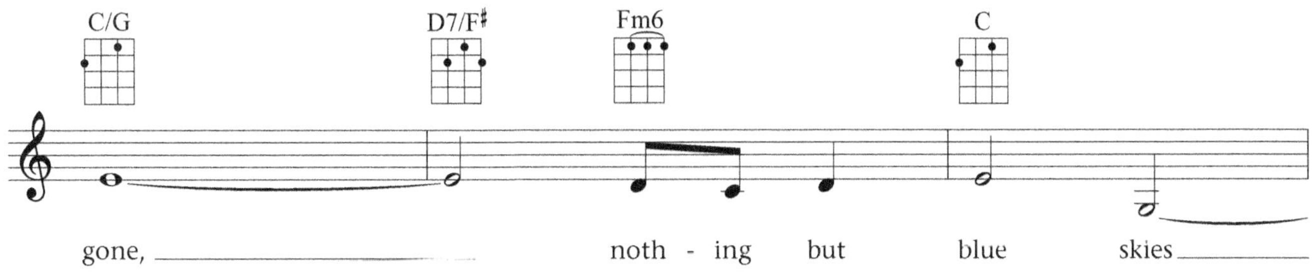
C/G
D7/F♯
Fm6
C
gone, noth - ing but blue skies

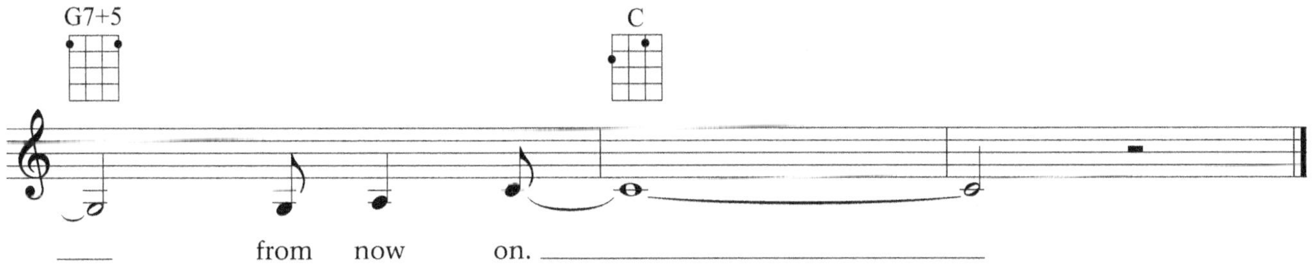
G7+5
C
from now on.

Bye Bye Blackbird

Words by
MORT DIXON

Music by
RAY HENDERSON

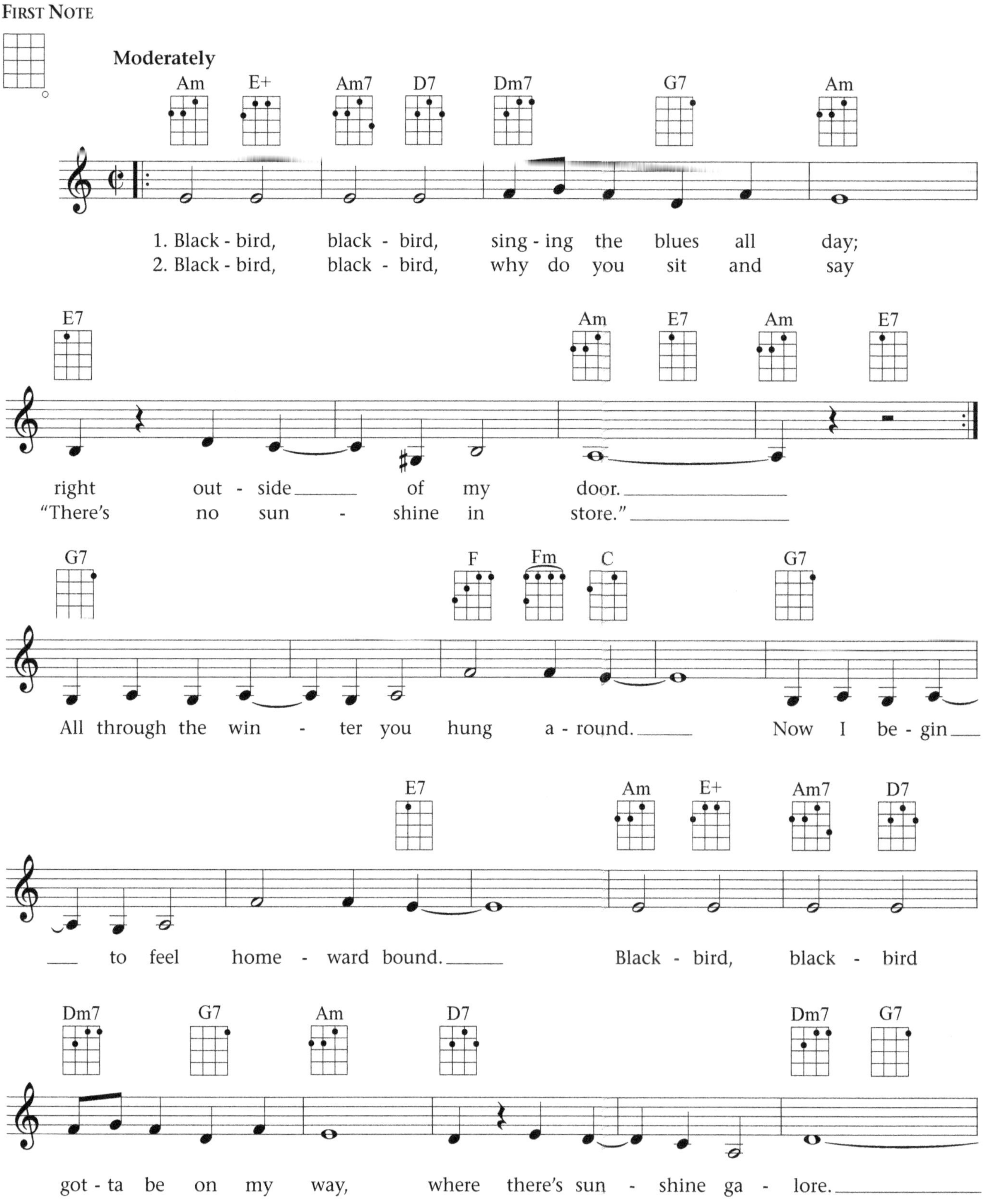

FIRST NOTE

Moderately

Am E+ Am7 D7 Dm7 G7 Am

1. Black - bird, black - bird, sing - ing the blues all day;
2. Black - bird, black - bird, why do you sit and say

E7 Am E7 Am E7

right out - side of my door.
"There's no sun - shine in store."

G7 F Fm C G7

All through the win - ter you hung a - round. Now I be - gin

E7 Am E+ Am7 D7

to feel home - ward bound. Black - bird, black - bird

Dm7 G7 Am D7 Dm7 G7

got - ta be on my way, where there's sun - shine ga - lore.

Dm7 G7 C F C Em G7
Pack up all my care and woe, here I go
Dm7 C F♯dim Dm7 G7 Dm7 G7
sing - ing low. Bye bye, black - bird.
Dm Dm(maj7) Dm7 G7 Em
Where some - bod - y waits for me, sug - ar's sweet,
G7 C C7
so is she. Bye bye, black - bird. No one here can
Gm7 C♯dim Dm Fm6 C D7
love and un - der - stand me. Oh, what hard luck stor - ies they all
F6 G7 C F C Em G7
hand me. Make my bed and light the light, I'll ar - rive
Gm6 A7 Dm G7 C F C
late to - night. Black - bird, bye bye.

The Christmas Song
(Chestnuts Roasting On An Open Fire)

Words and Music by
MEL TORME and ROBERT WELLS

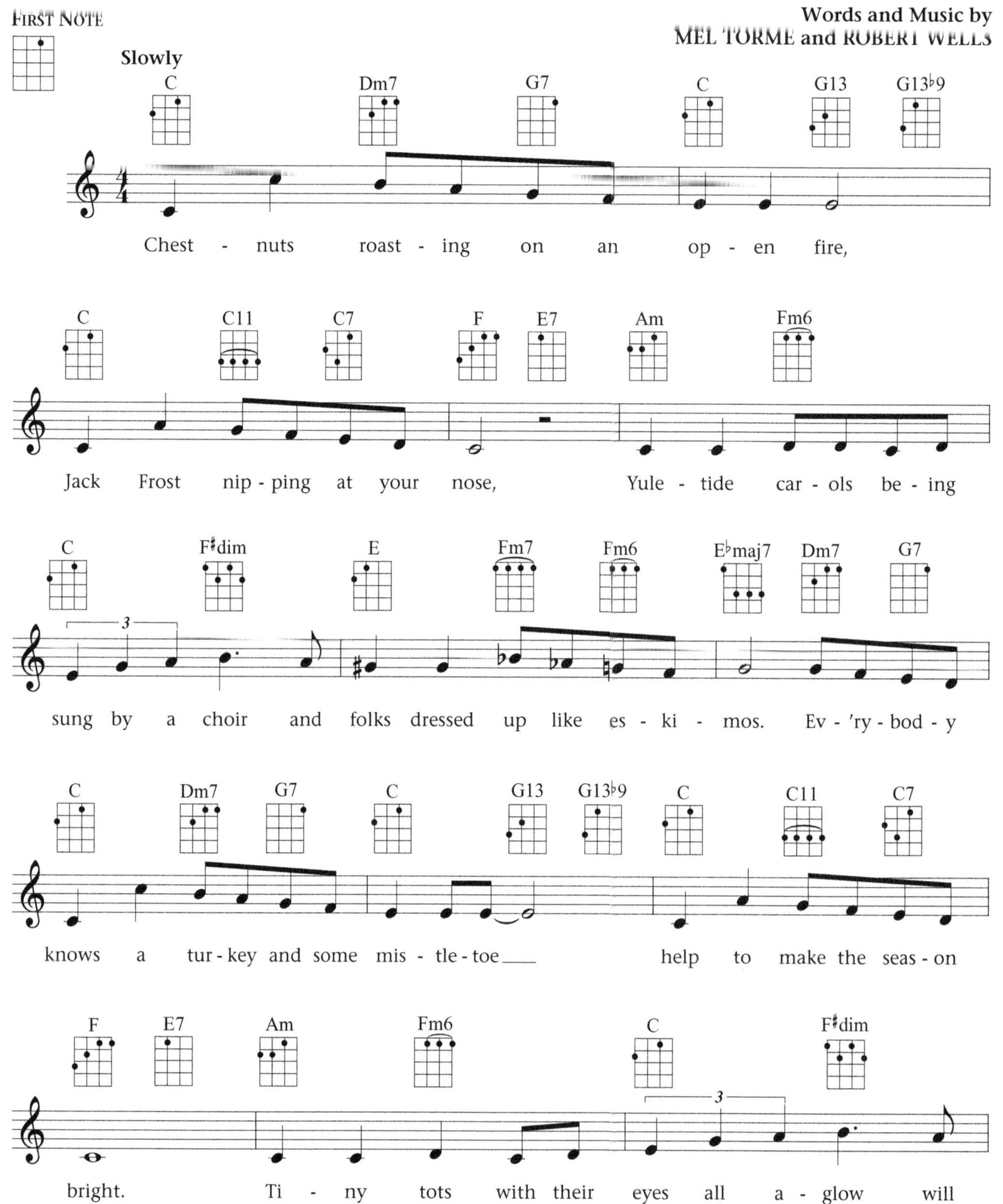

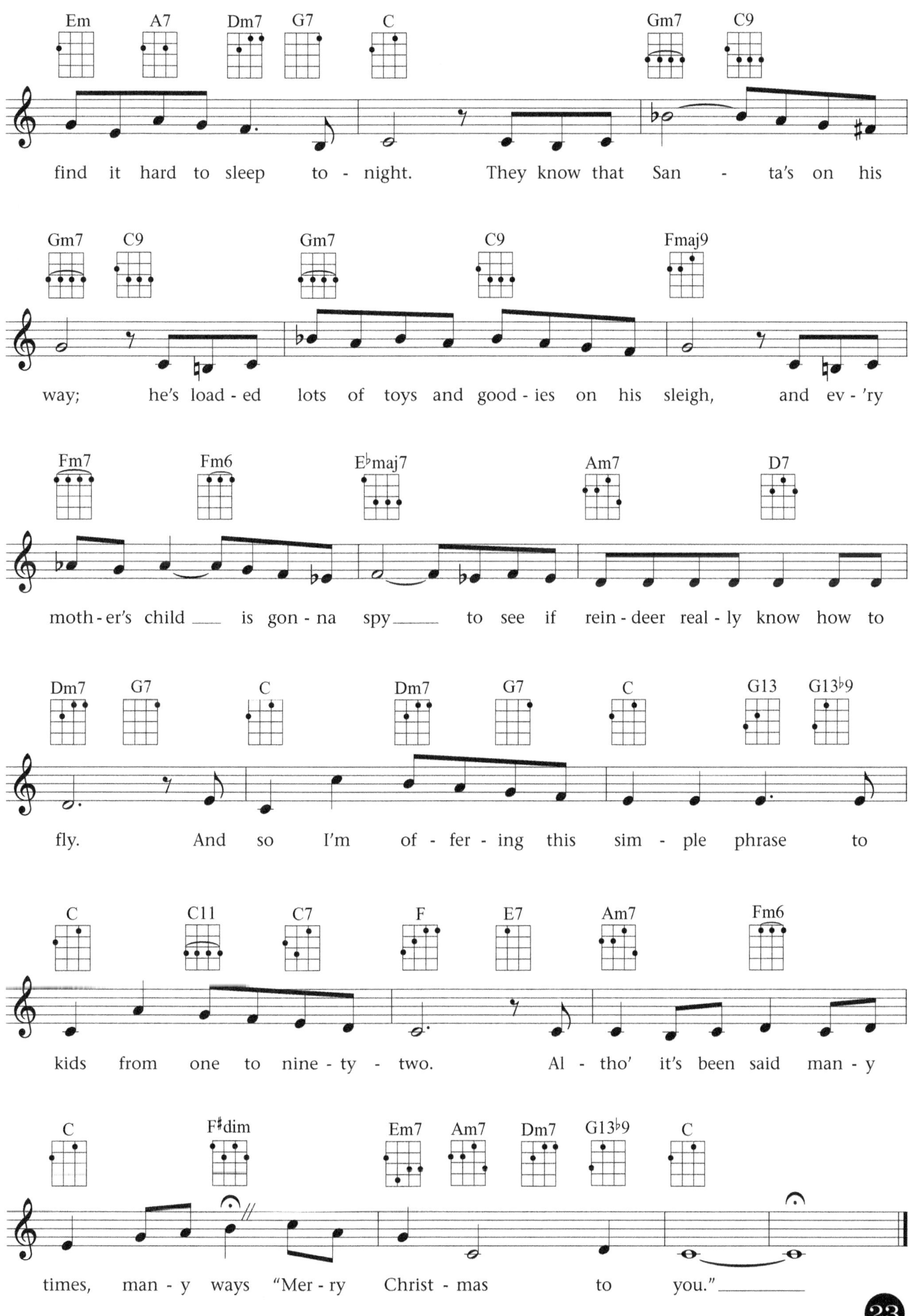
Em A7 Dm7 G7 C Gm7 C9
find it hard to sleep to - night. They know that San - ta's on his
Gm7 C9 Gm7 C9 Fmaj9
way; he's load - ed lots of toys and good - ies on his sleigh, and ev - 'ry
Fm7 Fm6 E♭maj7 Am7 D7
moth - er's child is gon - na spy to see if rein - deer real - ly know how to
Dm7 G7 C Dm7 G7 C G13 G13♭9
fly. And so I'm of - fer - ing this sim - ple phrase to
C C11 C7 F E7 Am7 Fm6
kids from one to nine - ty - two. Al - tho' it's been said man - y
C F♯dim Em7 Am7 Dm7 G13♭9 C
times, man - y ways "Mer - ry Christ - mas to you."

Crazy

First Note
Words and Music by
WILLIE NELSON
Moderately slow
C
A7
Dm
Dm(maj7)
Cra - zy, cra - zy for feel - in' so lone - ly,
Dm7
Dm6
G7
I'm cra - zy, cra - zy for feel - in' so
C
C♯dim
Dm7
G7
C
A7
blue. I knew you'd love me as long as you
Dm
Dm(maj7)
Dm7
Dm6
G7
want - ed, and then some - day you'd
C
F
C
C7
F
leave me for some - bod - y new. Wor - ry,

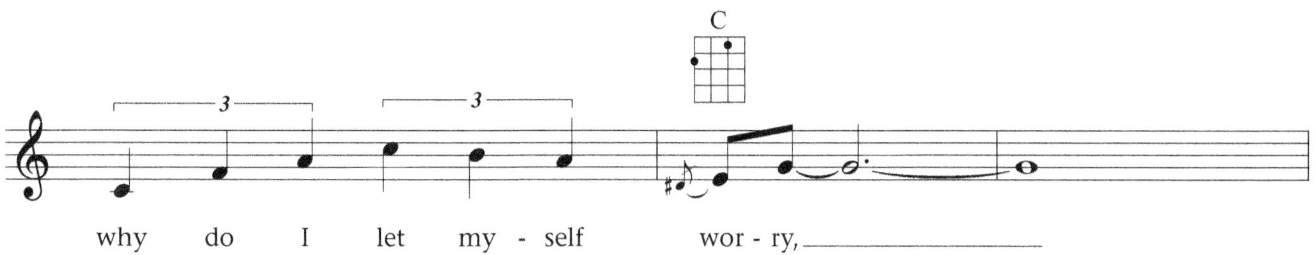
C
why do I let my - self wor - ry,

D7
G7
Dm7
won - d'rin'
what in the world did I do?

G7
C
A7
Cra - zy,
for think - ing that my love could
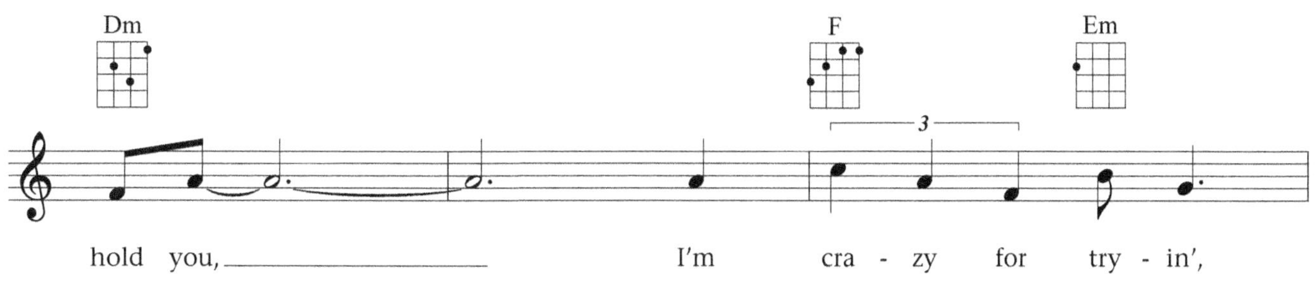
Dm
F
Em
hold you,
I'm cra - zy for try - in',
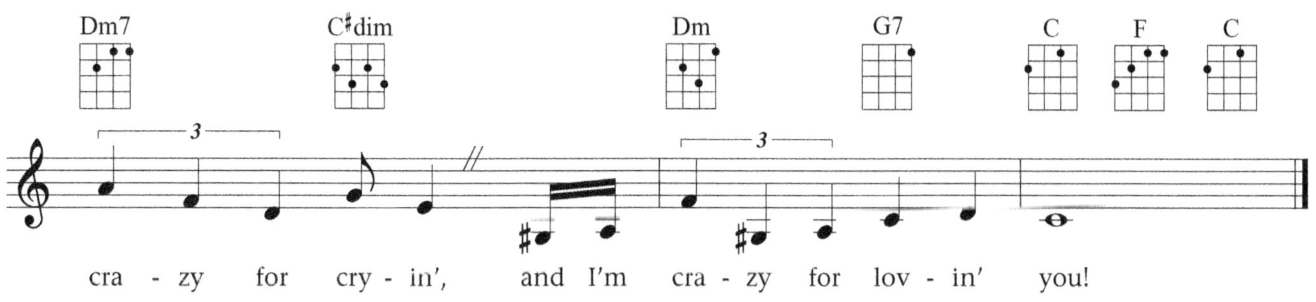
Dm7
C♯dim
Dm
G7
C
F
C
cra - zy for cry - in', and I'm cra - zy for lov - in' you!

Five Foot Two, Eyes Of Blue
(Has Anybody Seen My Girl?)

Words by
SAM LEWIS and JOE YOUNG

Music by
RAY HENDERSON

FIRST NOTE

Moderately

C E7 A7

Five foot two, eyes of blue, but oh! what those five

D7 G7

foot could do, ___ has an - y - bod - y seen my

C G+ C E7

girl? ___ Turned up nose, turned down hose,

A7 D7

nev - er had no oth - er beaus. ___ Has an - y - bod - y

G7 C

seen my girl? ___ Now if you

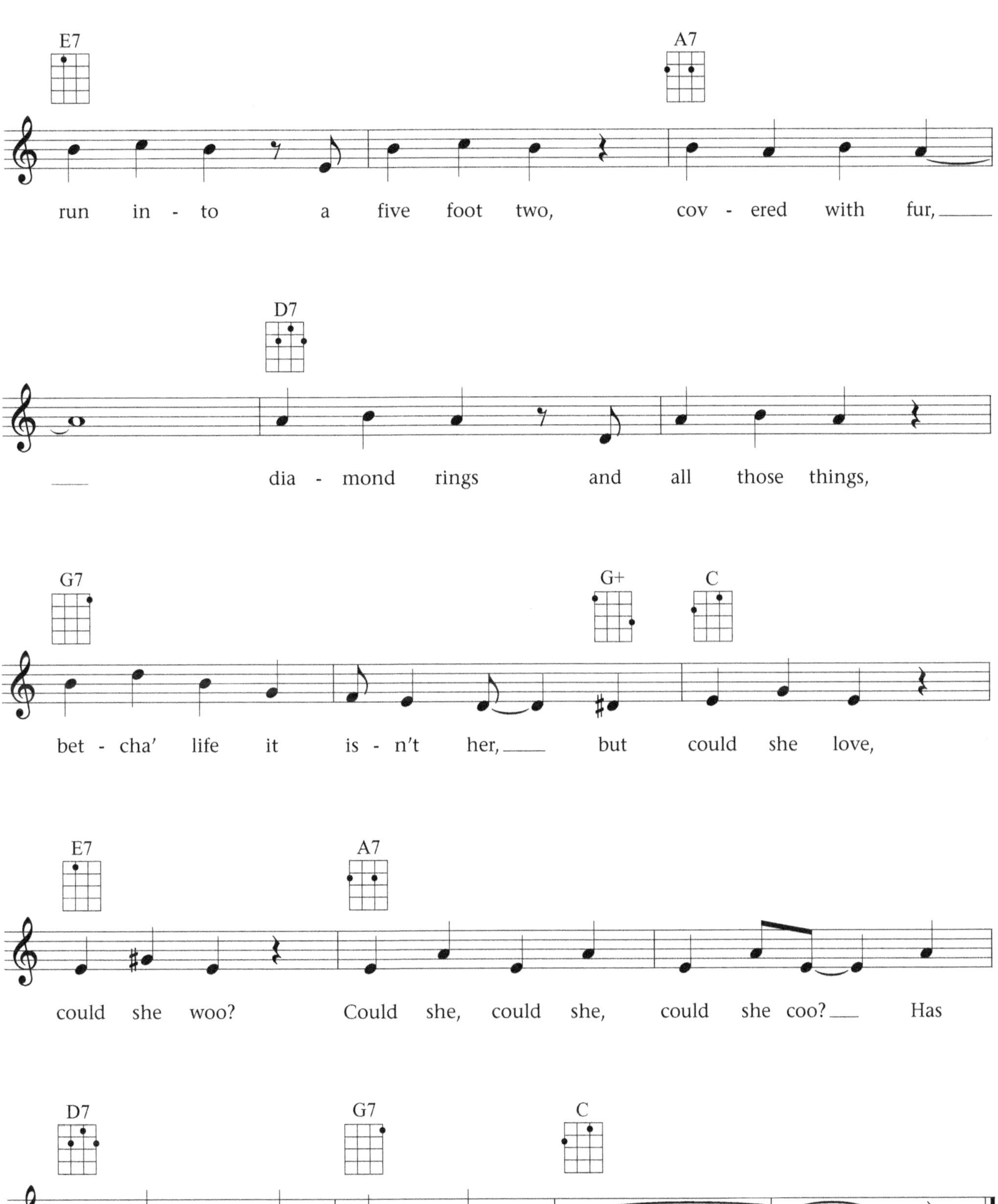
E7
A7
run in - to a five foot two, cov - ered with fur,
D7
dia - mond rings and all those things,
G7
G+
C
bet - cha' life it is - n't her, but could she love,
E7
A7
could she woo? Could she, could she, could she coo? Has
D7
G7
C
an - y - bod - y seen my girl?

Georgia On My Mind

Words by
STUART GORRELL

Music by
HOAGY CARMICHAEL

Am Dm Am F7 Am Dm
Oth - er arms reach out to me; oth - er eyes smile
Am7 D7 Am Dm
ten - der - ly; still in peace - ful
Am7 B7 Em C♯dim
dreams I see, the road leads back to
Dm7 G7 C E7
you. Geor - gia, Geor - gia,
Am Dm7 Fm6 C B7
no peace I find, just an old sweet song keeps
Dm7 D9 G7 C F6 G7+5 C6/9
Geor - gia on my mind.

Heart And Soul

Words by
FRANK LOESSER

Music by
HOAGY CARMICHAEL

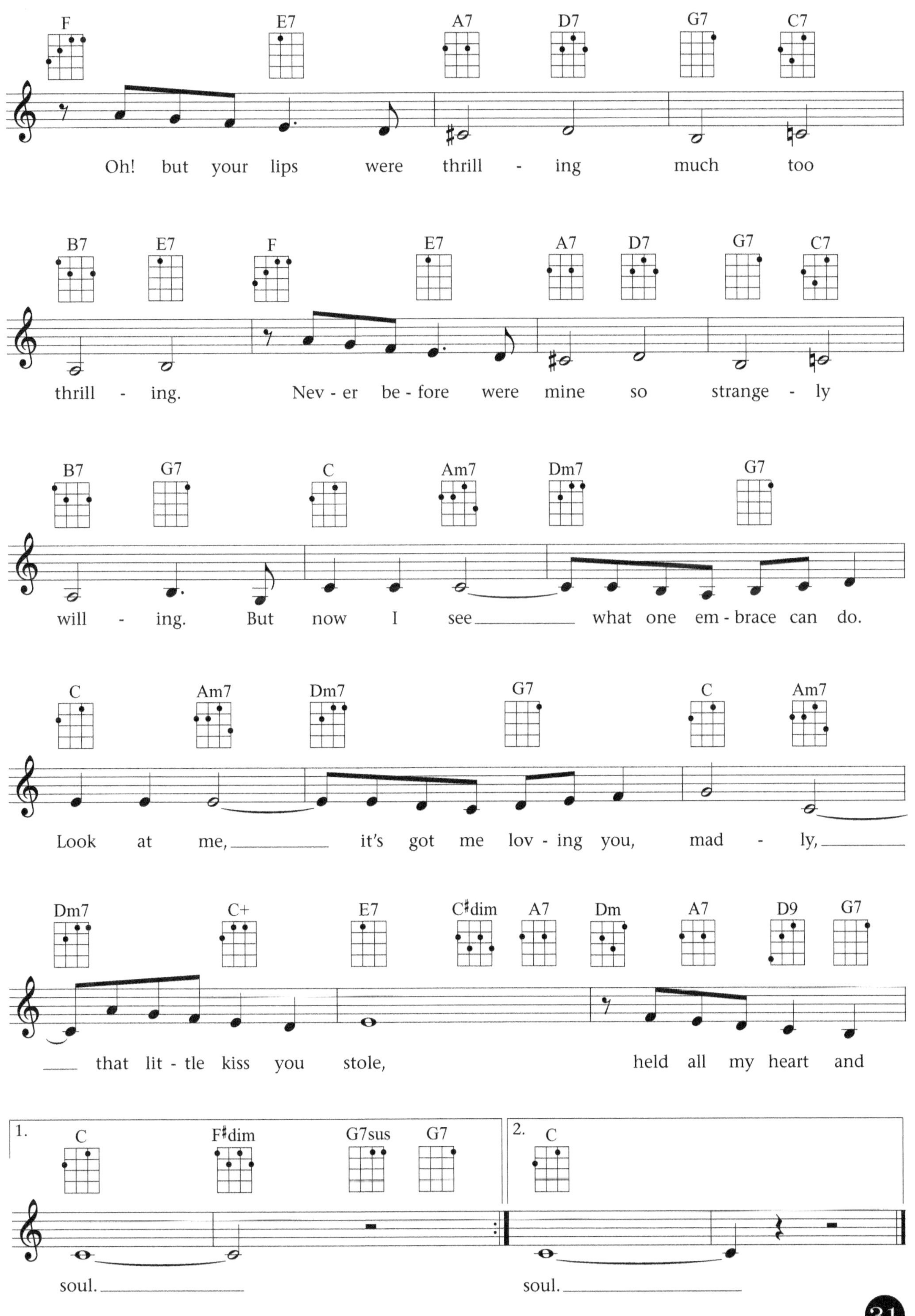
F E7 A7 D7 G7 C7
Oh! but your lips were thrill - ing much too
B7 E7 F E7 A7 D7 G7 C7
thrill - ing. Nev - er be - fore were mine so strange - ly
B7 G7 C Am7 Dm7 G7
will - ing. But now I see what one em - brace can do.
C Am7 Dm7 G7 C Am7
Look at me, it's got me lov - ing you, mad - ly,
Dm7 C+ E7 C♯dim A7 Dm A7 D9 G7
that lit - tle kiss you stole, held all my heart and
1. C F♯dim G7sus G7
soul.
2. C
soul.

Home On The Range

FIRST NOTE

Traditional

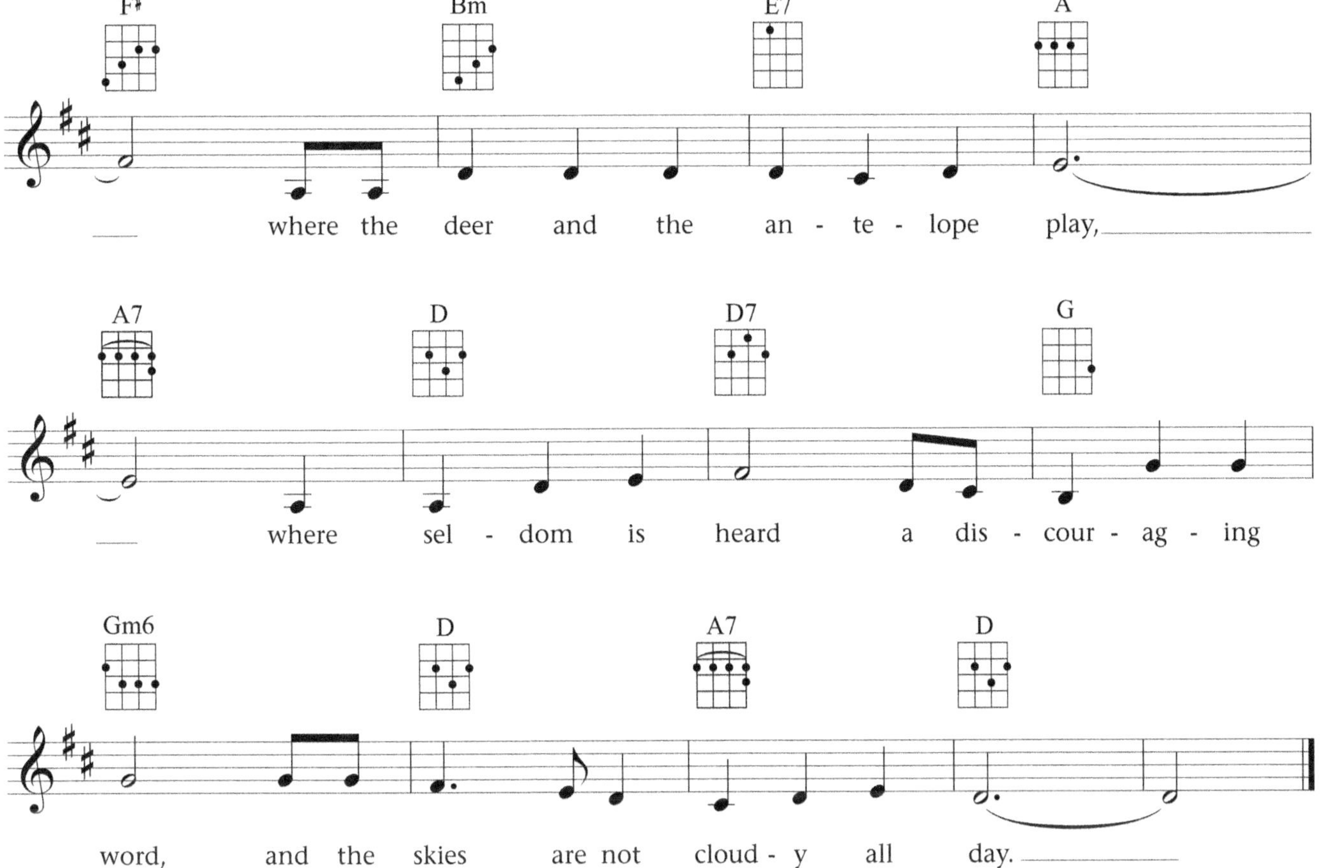

Additional Lyrics

2. Oh, give me a land where the bright diamond sand
flows leisurely down the clear stream;
where the graceful white swan goes gliding along
like a maid in a heavenly dream.
CHORUS

3. How often at night, when the heavens are bright
with the light from the glittering stars,
have I stood there amazed and asked as I gazed
if their glory exceeds that of ours.
CHORUS

4. Where the air is so pure, and the zephyrs so free,
and the breezes so balmy and light,
that I would not exchange my home on the range
for all of the cities so bright.
CHORUS

I Don't Want To Set The World On Fire

Words by EDDIE SEILER
and SOL MARCUS

Music by BENNIE BENJAMIN
and EDDIE DURHAM

F
I just want to be the one you love. And
Am7 D9 Am7 D9
with your ad - mis - sion that you feel the same.
Dm7 G7 G+
3
I'll have reached the goal I'm dream - ing of, be - lieve me!
C E♭dim Dm7
I don't want to set the world on fire,
Fm6 G9
I just want to start a flame in your heart.
C B♭6 B6 C6

I'll See You In My Dreams

Words by
GUS KAHN

Music by
ISHAM JONES

F
Fm6
Lips that once were mine,

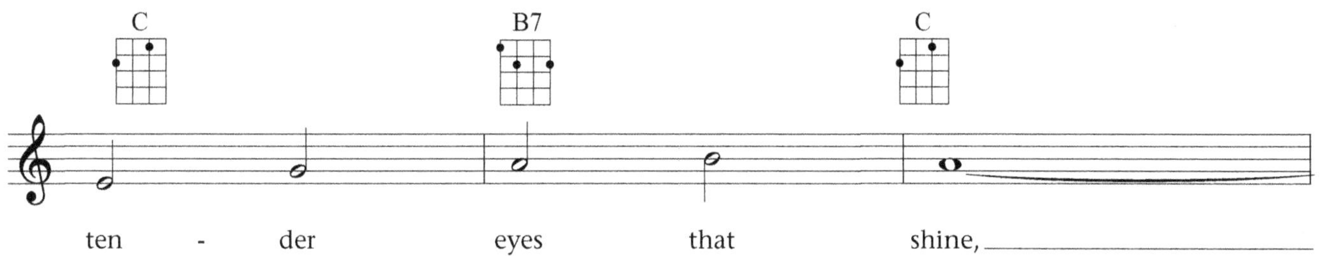
C
B7
C
ten - der eyes that shine,

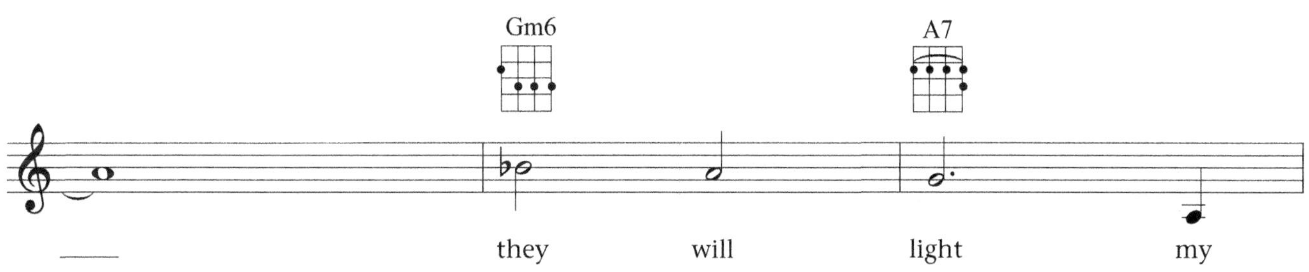
Gm6
A7
they will light my

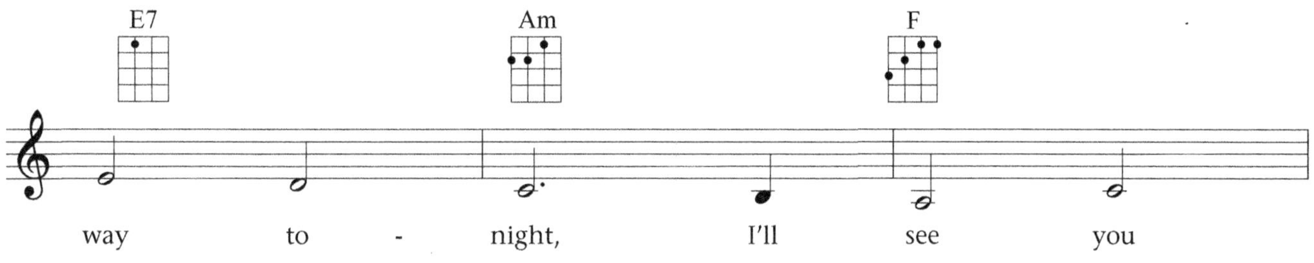
E7
Am
F
way to - night, I'll see you

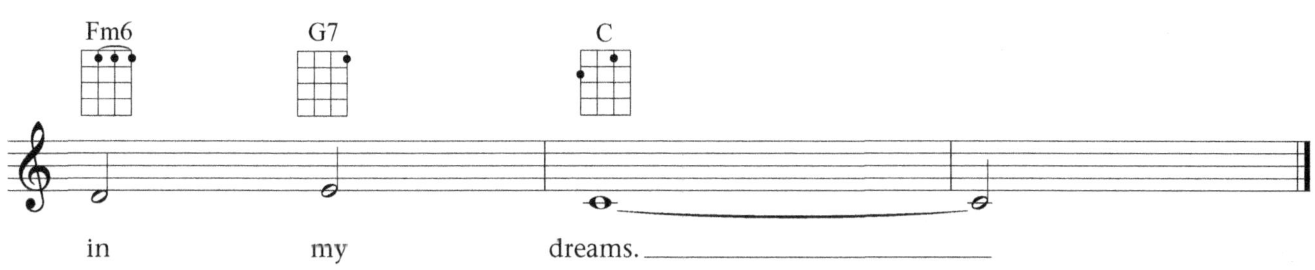
Fm6
G7
C
in my dreams.

It Had To Be You

Words by
GUS KAHN

Music by
ISHAM JONES

FIRST NOTE

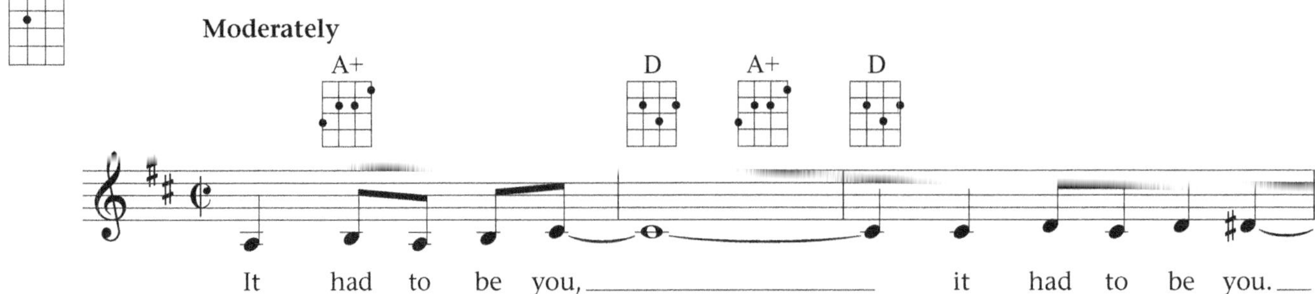

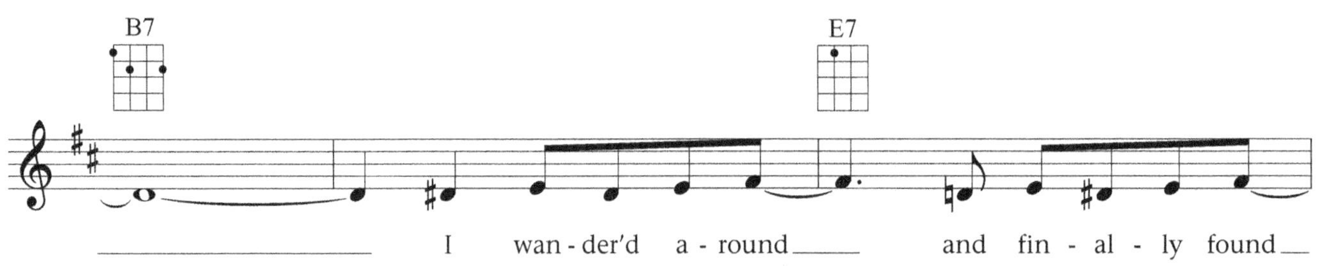

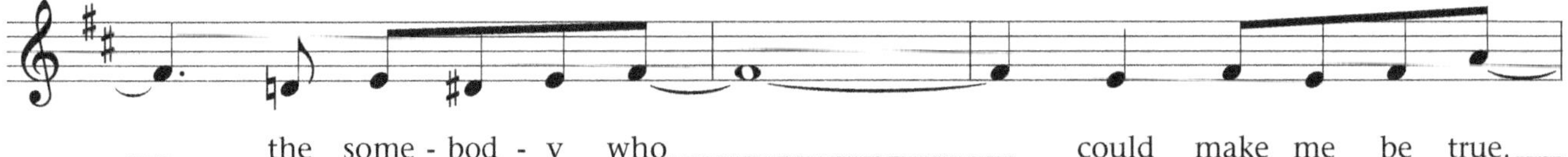

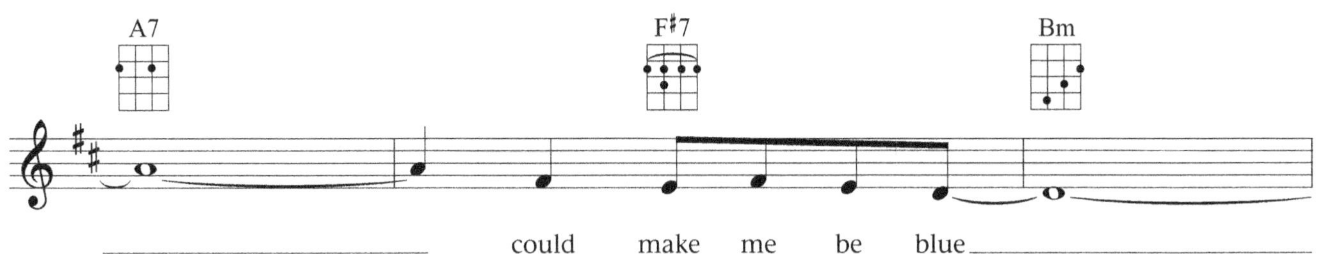

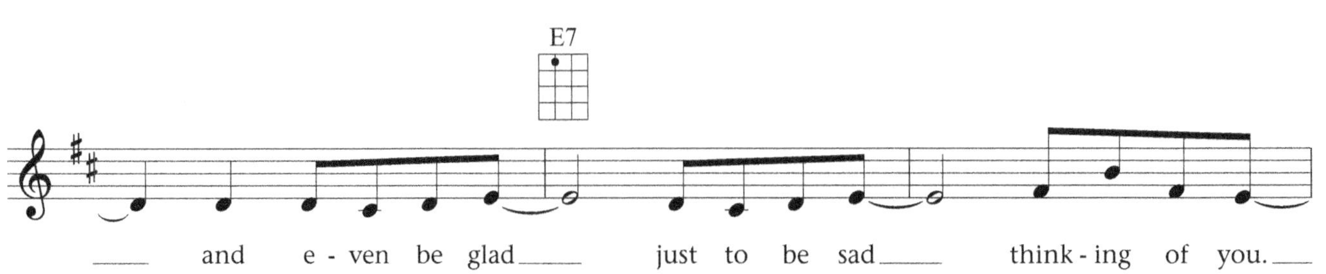

A7
A+
D
A+
Some oth - ers I've seen
D
B7
might nev - er be mean.
Might nev - er be cross
E7
or try to be boss,
but they would - n't do.
Bm
Em
For no - bod - y else
gave me a thrill,
Edim
A7
D
F♯7
Bm
Bdim
with all your faults
I love you still.
It had to be you,
A7
Bdim
A7
D
won - der - ful you,
had to be you.

King Of The Road

Words and Music by
ROGER MILLER

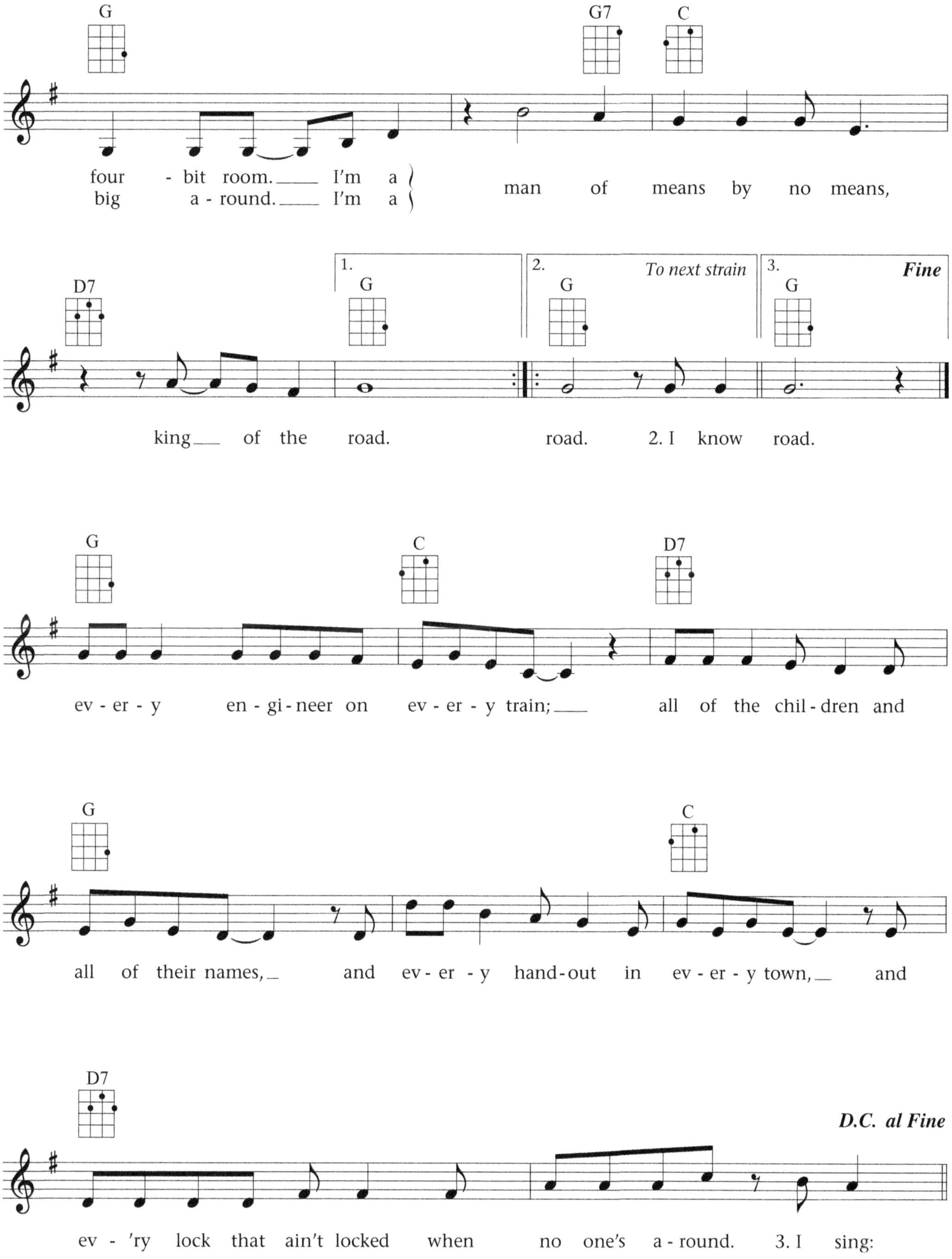

G G7 C

four - bit room. I'm a
big a - round. I'm a
man of means by no means,

D7 1. G 2. G *To next strain* 3. G ***Fine***

king of the road. road. 2. I know road.

G C D7

ev - er - y en - gi - neer on ev - er - y train; all of the chil - dren and

Lullaby Of Birdland

Words by
GEORGE DAVID WEISS

Music by
GEORGE SHEARING

FIRST NOTE

Moderately slow

Bm G♯7♭5 C♯7♭9 F♯7♭9 Bm7 Gmaj7

Lul - la - by of Bird - land that's what I ___ al - ways hear ___

Em7 A9 F♯m7 Bm7 Em7 A7♭9

when you sigh. ___ Nev - er in my word - land could there be ways ___ to re - veal, ___

D G9 C♯m7♭5 F♯7 Bm F♯m7♭5

___ in a phrase, ___ how I feel! ___ Have you ev - er heard two

C♯7♭9 F♯7♭9 Bm7 Gmaj7 Em7 A9

tur - tle doves ___ bill and coo ___ when they love? ___

F♯m7 Bm7 Em7 A7♭9 D A7

That's the kind of mag - ic mus - ic we make ___ with our lips ___ when we kiss! ___

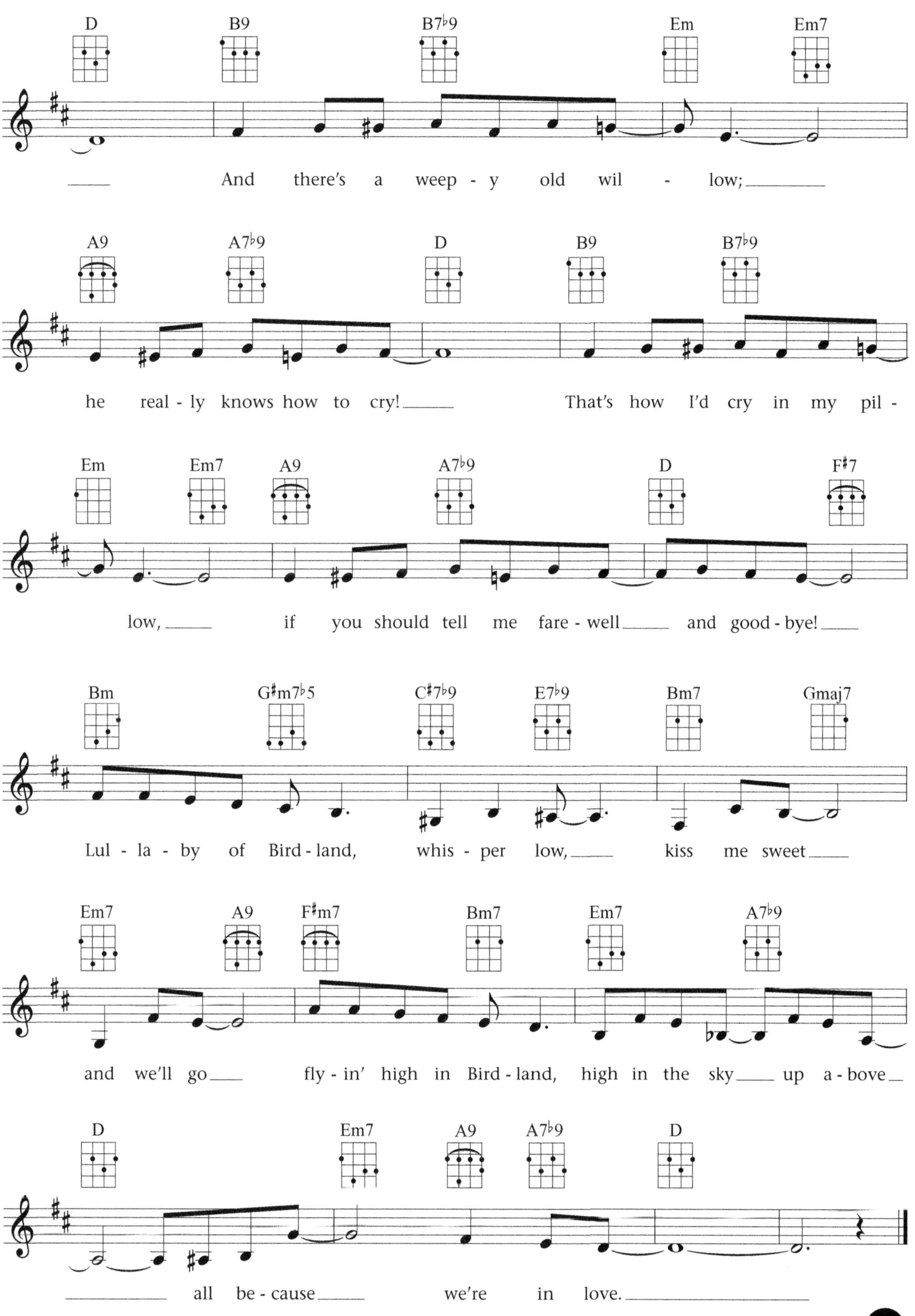
D
B9
B7♭9
Em
Em7
And there's a weep - y old wil - low;
A9
A7♭9
D
B9
B7♭9
he real - ly knows how to cry!
That's how I'd cry in my pil -
Em
Em7
A9
A7♭9
D
F♯7
low,
if you should tell me fare - well
and good - bye!
Bm
G♯m7♭5
C♯7♭9
E7♭9
Bm7
Gmaj7
Lul - la - by of Bird - land,
whis - per low,
kiss me sweet
Em7
A9
F♯m7
Bm7
Em7
A7♭9
and we'll go
fly - in' high in Bird - land,
high in the sky
up a - bove
D
Em7
A9
A7♭9
D
all be - cause
we're in love.

Makin' Love Ukulele Style

Words by
CHARLIE HAYES

Music by
PAUL WEIRICK

D7 G
ev - 'ry note your heart will float far a -
G D7 G G+ C A7
way to a trop - ic isle while a
D7 G
u - ku - le - le tune is soft - ly played. Stroll - ing a -
C Cm G G7
long be - neath the star - light, dream - ing a
C Cm G
lov - er's dream for two. Soon you will
A7
see her his eyes are star - bright as the

Am7
D7
u - ku - le - le mag - ic comes through.
Now if
G
G7
C
D7
you want to sat - is - fy the one you love all
G
G
D7
G
G+
else a - bove, take a tip and be
C
A7
D7
sure you try the u - ku - le - le style of mak - in'
G
C♯dim
D7
love. Try the u - ku - le - le style of mak - in'
G
C♯dim
D7
G
love. Try the u - ku - le - le style of mak - in' love.

My Little Grass Shack In Kealakekua, Hawaii

Words and Music by
BILL COGSWELL, TOMMY HARRISON
and JOHNNY NOBLE

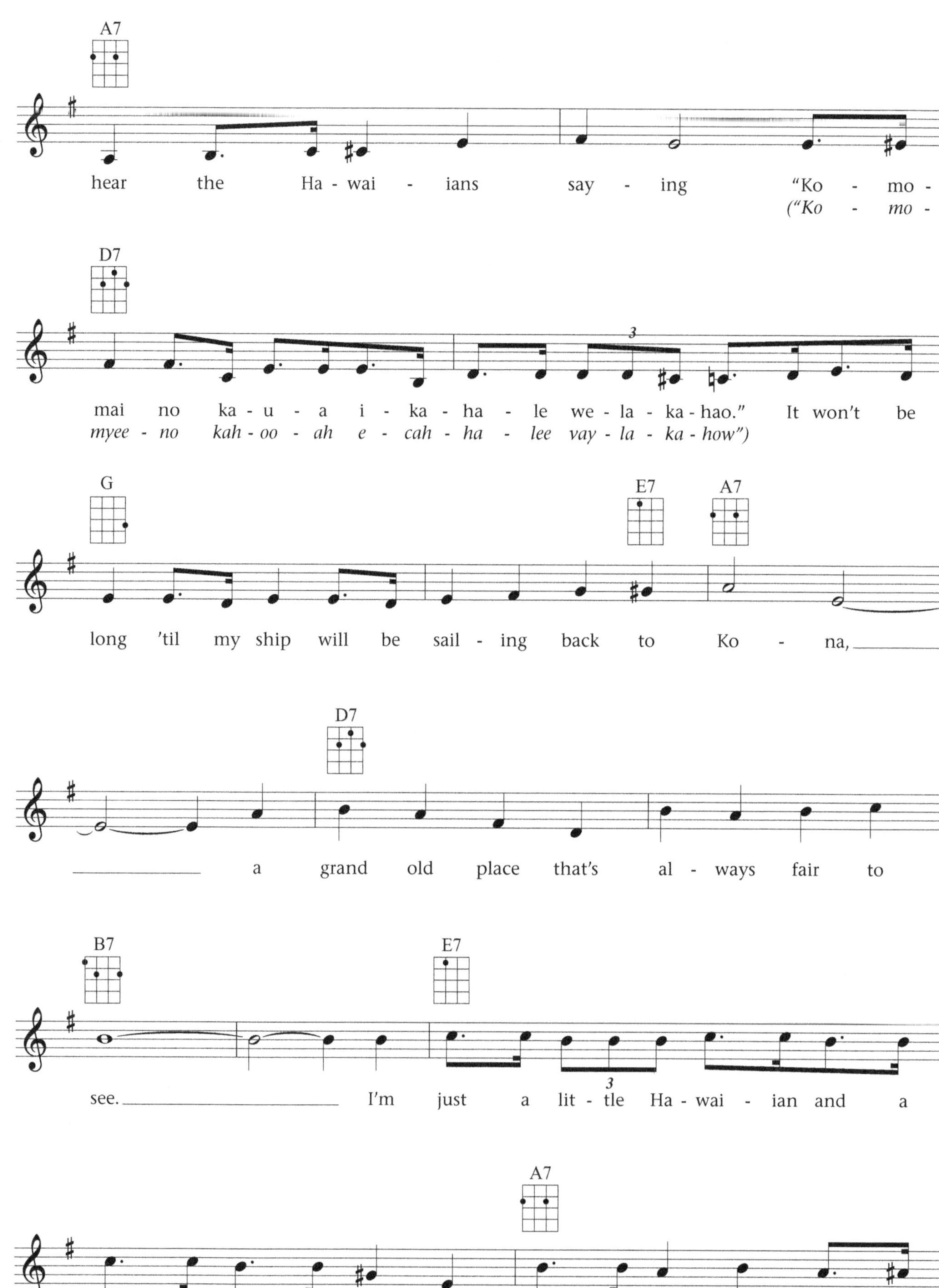
A7
hear the Ha - wai - ians say - ing "Ko - mo -
("Ko - mo -
D7
mai no ka - u - a i - ka - ha - le we - la - ka - hao." It won't be
myee - no kah - oo - ah e - cah - ha - lee vay - la - ka - how")
3
G
E7
A7
long 'til my ship will be sail - ing back to Ko - na,
D7
a grand old place that's al - ways fair to
B7
E7
see. I'm just a lit - tle Ha - wai - ian and a
3
A7
home - sick is - land boy, I want to go back to my

C♯dim G
fish and poi. I want to go back to my lit - tle grass
(poy)
E7 A7
shack in Ke - a - la - ke - kua, Ha - wai - i,
(Ke - ah - la - ke - kuah,)
D7
where the Hu - mu - hu - mu, Nu - ku - nu - ku
(Hoo - moo - hoo - moo, Noo - koo - noo - koo
G
a pu - a - a goes swim - ming by.
ah poo - ah - ah)
D7
Where the Hu - mu - hu - mu, Nu - ku - nu - ku
(Hoo - moo - hoo - moo, Noo - koo - noo - koo
G
a pu - a - a goes swim - ming by.
ah poo - ah - ah)

Mele Kalikimaka

FIRST NOTE

Words and Music by
ALEX ANDERSON

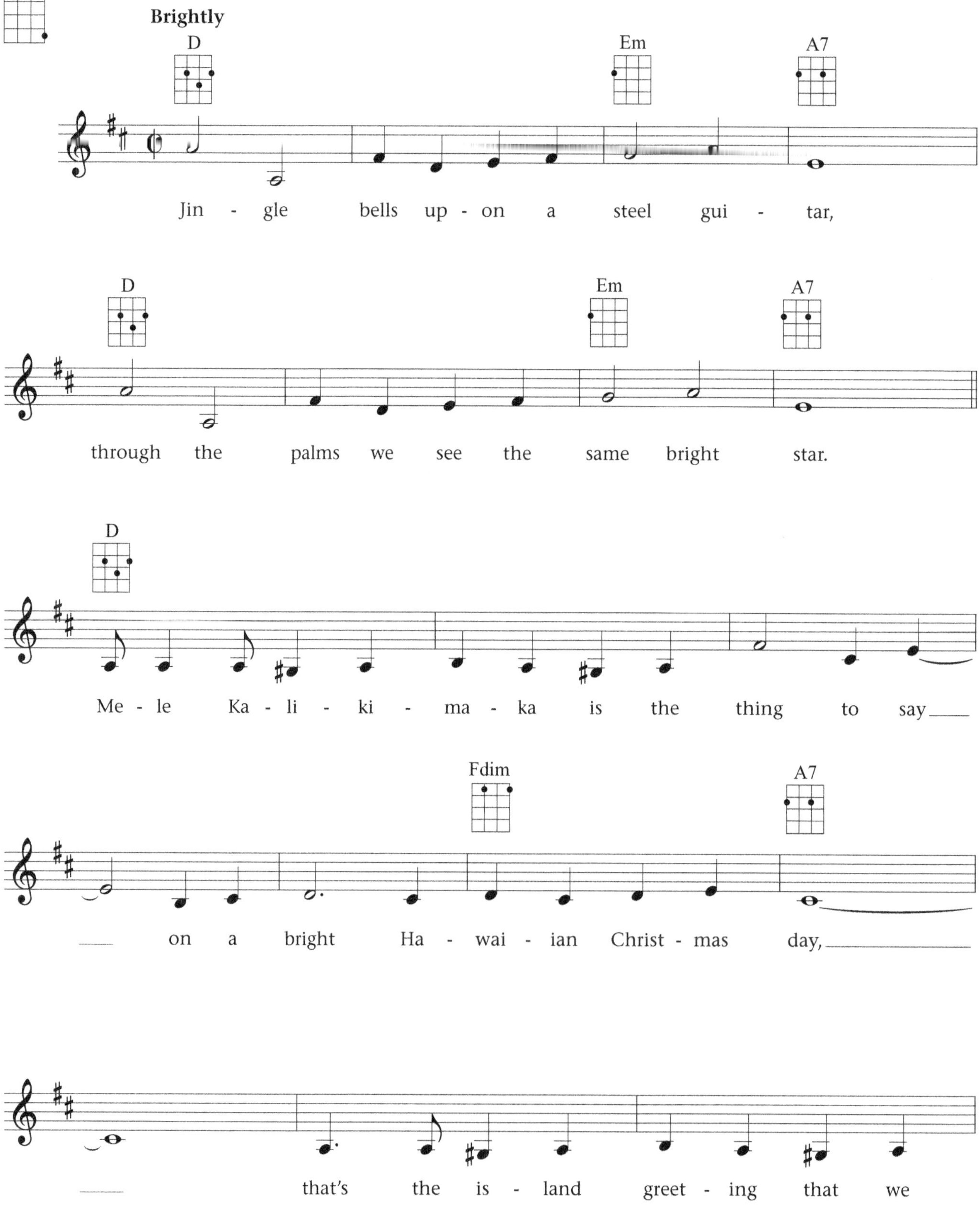

Brightly

D Em A7

Jin - gle bells up - on a steel gui - tar,

D Em A7

through the palms we see the same bright star.

D

Me - le Ka - li - ki - ma - ka is the thing to say

Fdim A7

on a bright Ha - wai - ian Christ - mas day,

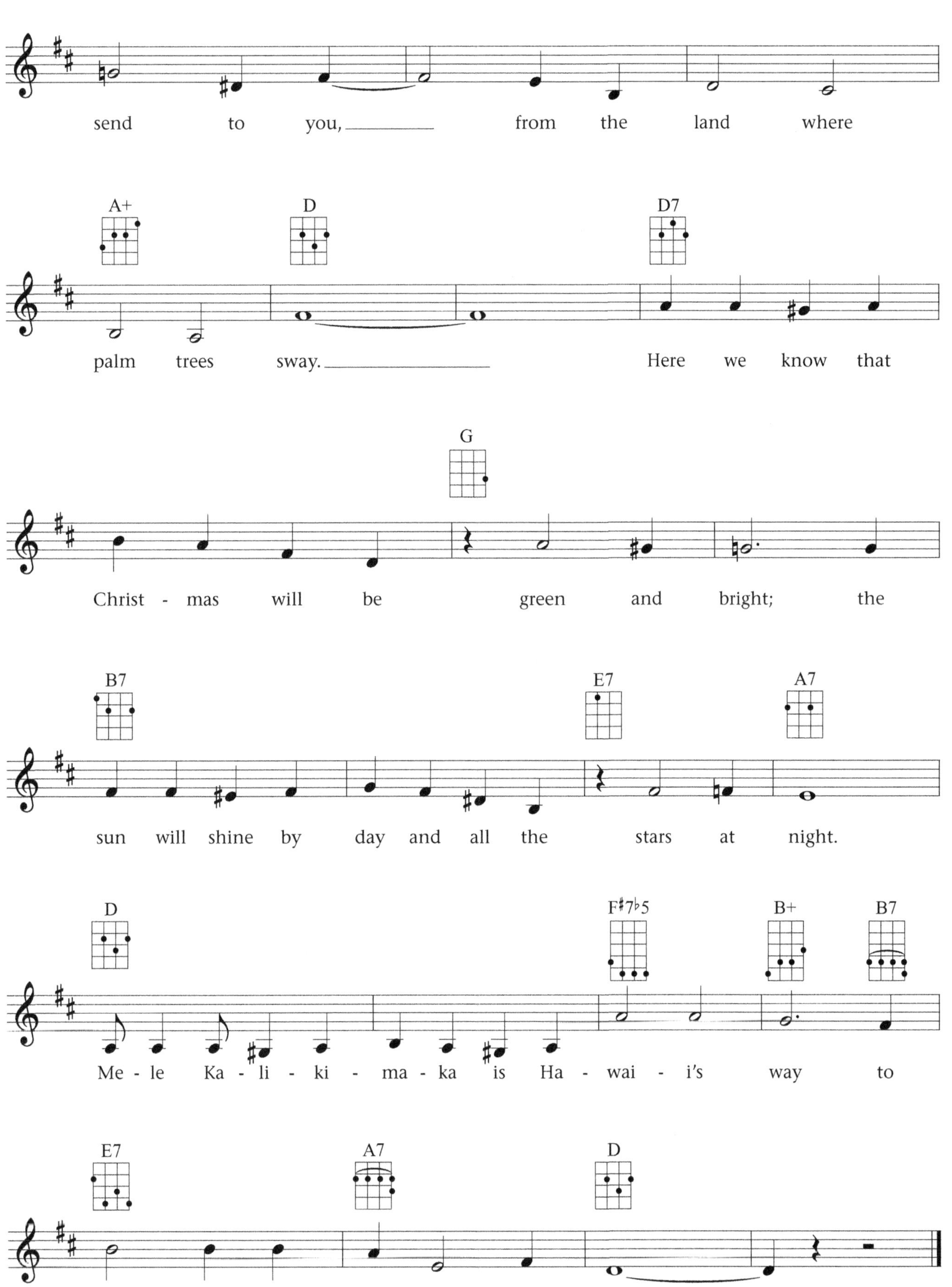
send to you, from the land where
A+
D
D7
palm trees sway. Here we know that
G
Christ - mas will be green and bright; the
B7
E7
A7
sun will shine by day and all the stars at night.
D
F♯7♭5
B+
B7
Me - le Ka - li - ki - ma - ka is Ha - wai - i's way to
E7
A7
D
say Mer - ry Christ - mas to you.

Moon River

Words by
JOHNNY MERCER
Music by
HENRY MANCINI
FIRST NOTE
Slowly
G Em C
Moon Riv - er wid - er than a
G C G
mile; I'm cross - ing you in style some
F♯m7♭5 B7 Em G7
day. Old dream - mak - er, you
C F9 Em Em7
heart - break - er, wher - ev - er you're
C♯m7♭5 F♯7 Bm7 E7 Am7 D9
go - in', I'm go - in' your way.

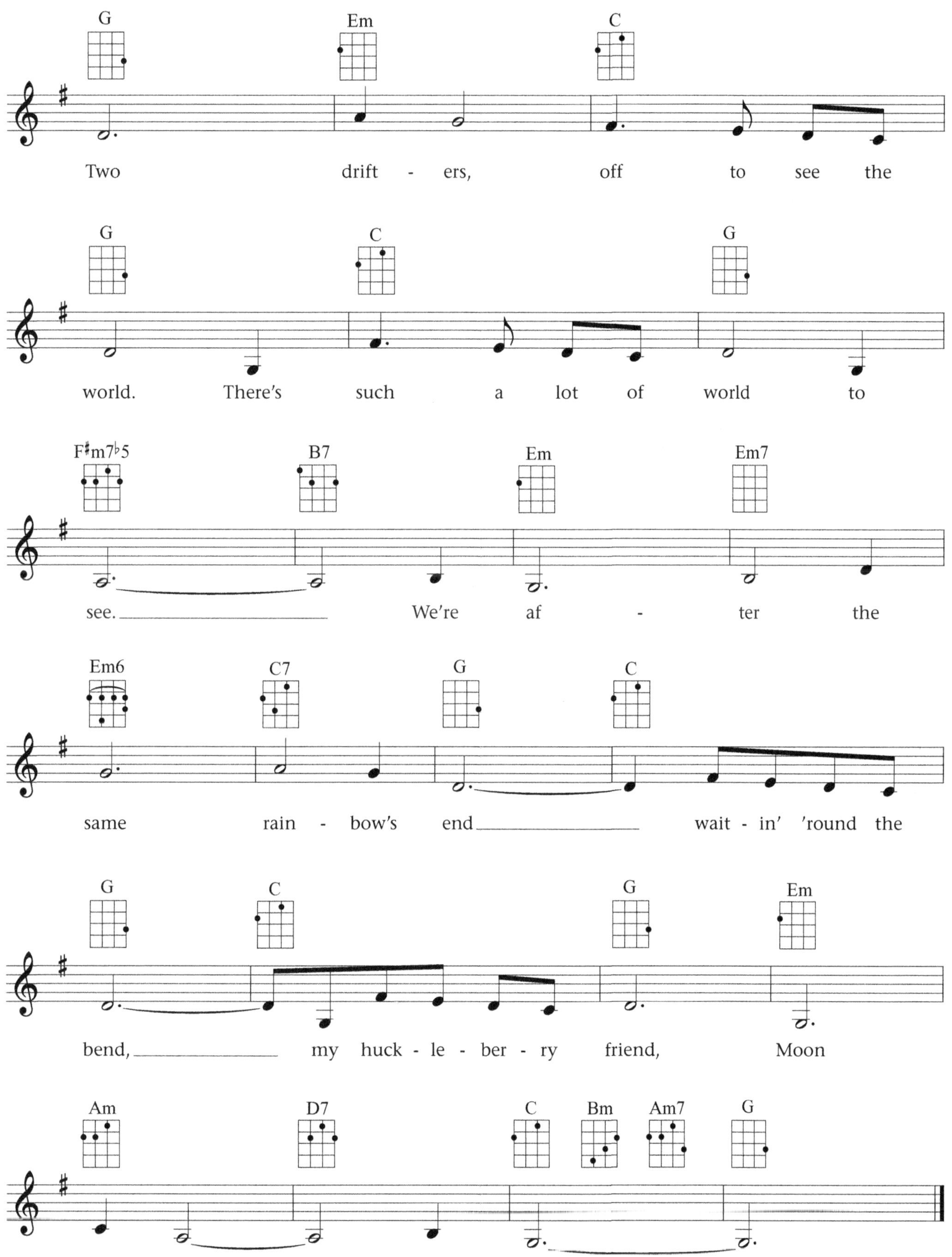
G
Em
C
Two drift - ers, off to see the
G
C
G
world. There's such a lot of world to
F♯m7♭5
B7
Em
Em7
see. We're af - ter the
Em6
C7
G
C
same rain - bow's end wait - in' 'round the
G
C
G
Em
bend, my huck - le - ber - ry friend, Moon
Am
D7
C
Bm
Am7
G
Riv - er and me.

On A Slow Boat To China

Words and Music by
FRANK LOESSER

FIRST NOTE

C7
F
Am
D7
Gm7
Out on the bri - ny with a moon big and
G♯dim
F
A7
shi - ny, melt - ing your heart of
B♭
D7
Gm7
E♭7
stone, I'd love to get you, on a
F
D7
G7
Gm7
C7
slow boat to Chi - na, all to my - self a -
F
Fine
lone. There is no verse to this song
D.C. al Fine
B♭
F
B♭
C7
'cause I don't want to wait a mo - ment too long to say that

Over The Rainbow

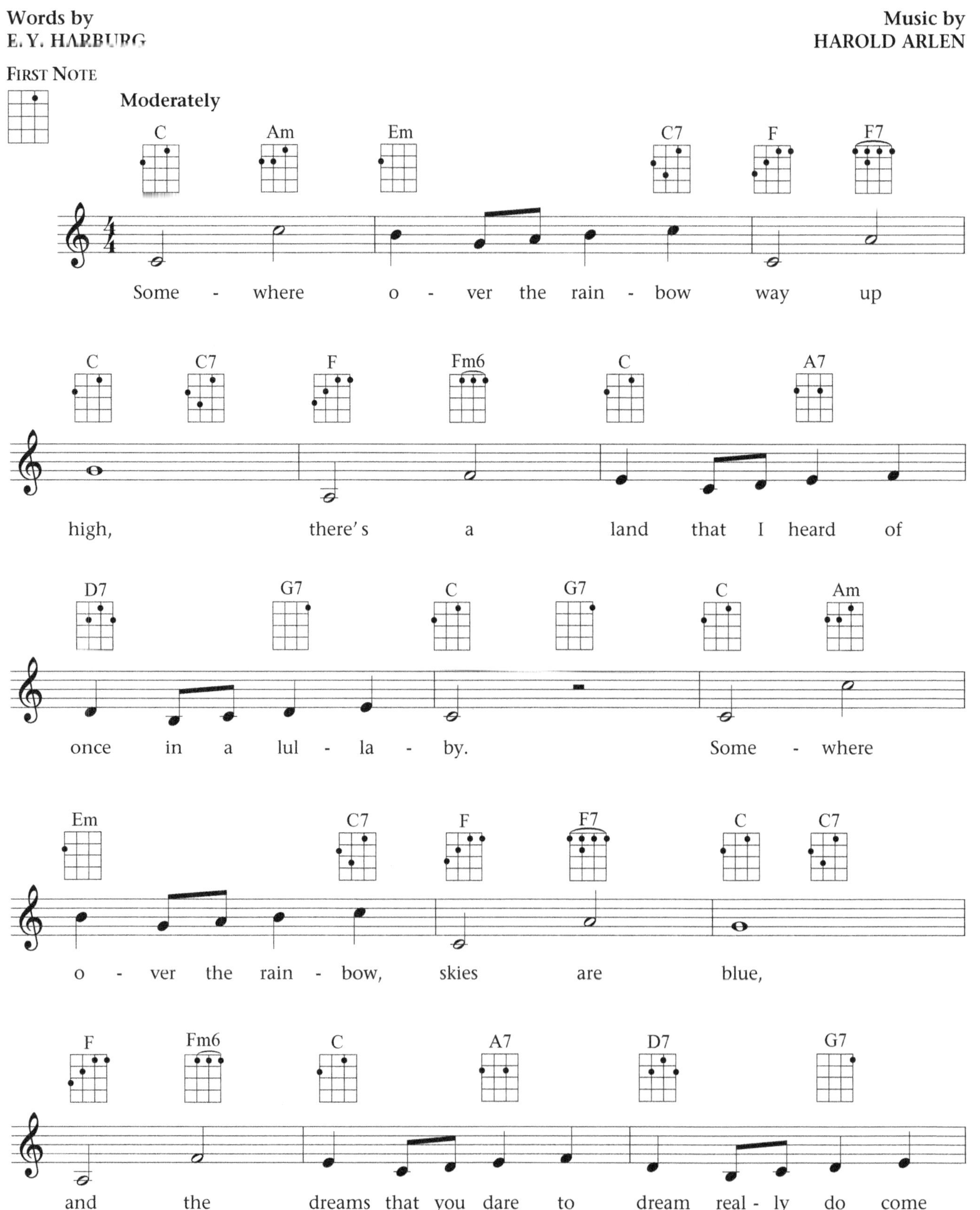

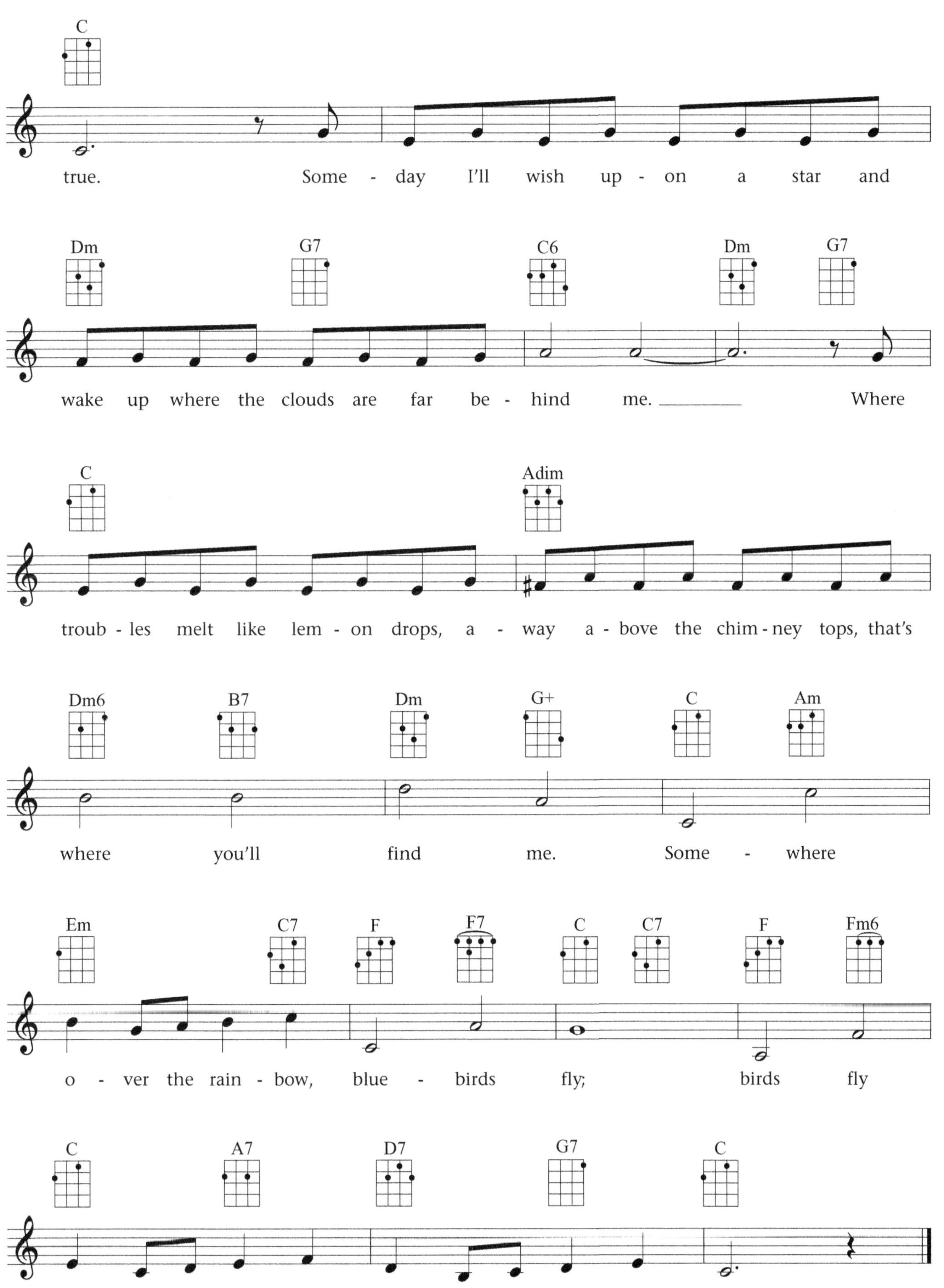
C
true. Some - day I'll wish up - on a star and
Dm G7 C6 Dm G7
wake up where the clouds are far be - hind me. Where
C Adim
troub - les melt like lem - on drops, a - way a - bove the chim - ney tops, that's
Dm6 B7 Dm G+ C Am
where you'll find me. Some - where
Em C7 F F7 C C7 F Fm6
o - ver the rain - bow, blue - birds fly; birds fly
C A7 D7 G7 C
o - ver the rain - bow, why then, oh why can't I?

Pennies From Heaven

Words by
JOHN BURKE

Music by
ARTHUR JOHNSTON

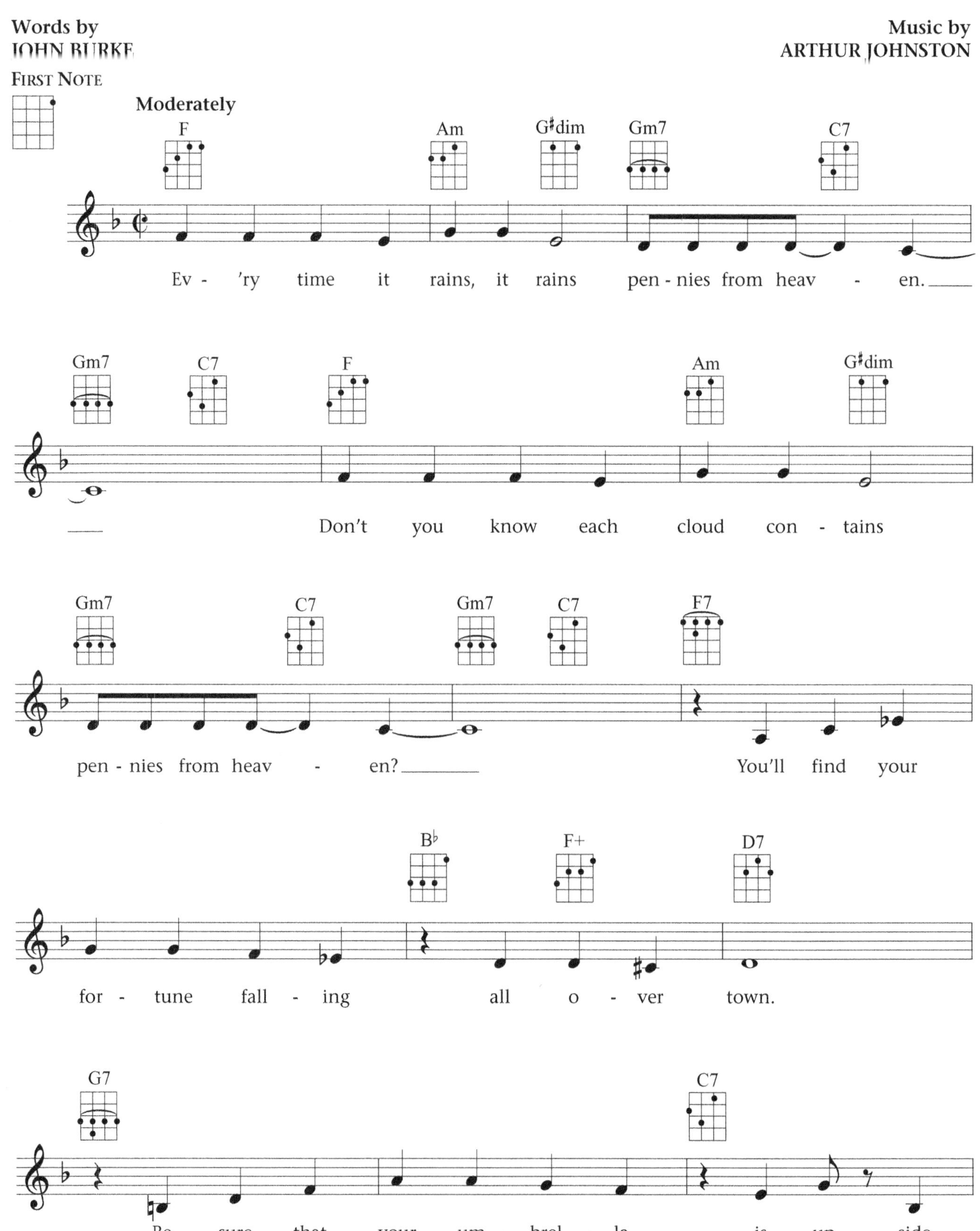

C+
F
Am
G♯dim
down. Trade them for a pack - age of
Gm7
C7
Gm7
C7
F7
sun - shine and flow - ers.
If you want the
B♭
things you love, you must have show - ers.
E♭7
F
So when you hear it thun - der, don't run un - der a tree,
D9
Gm7
there'll be pen - nies from heav - en for
G7
C7
F
you and me.

Raindrops Keep Fallin' On My Head

Words by
HAL DAVID

Music by
BURT BACHARACH

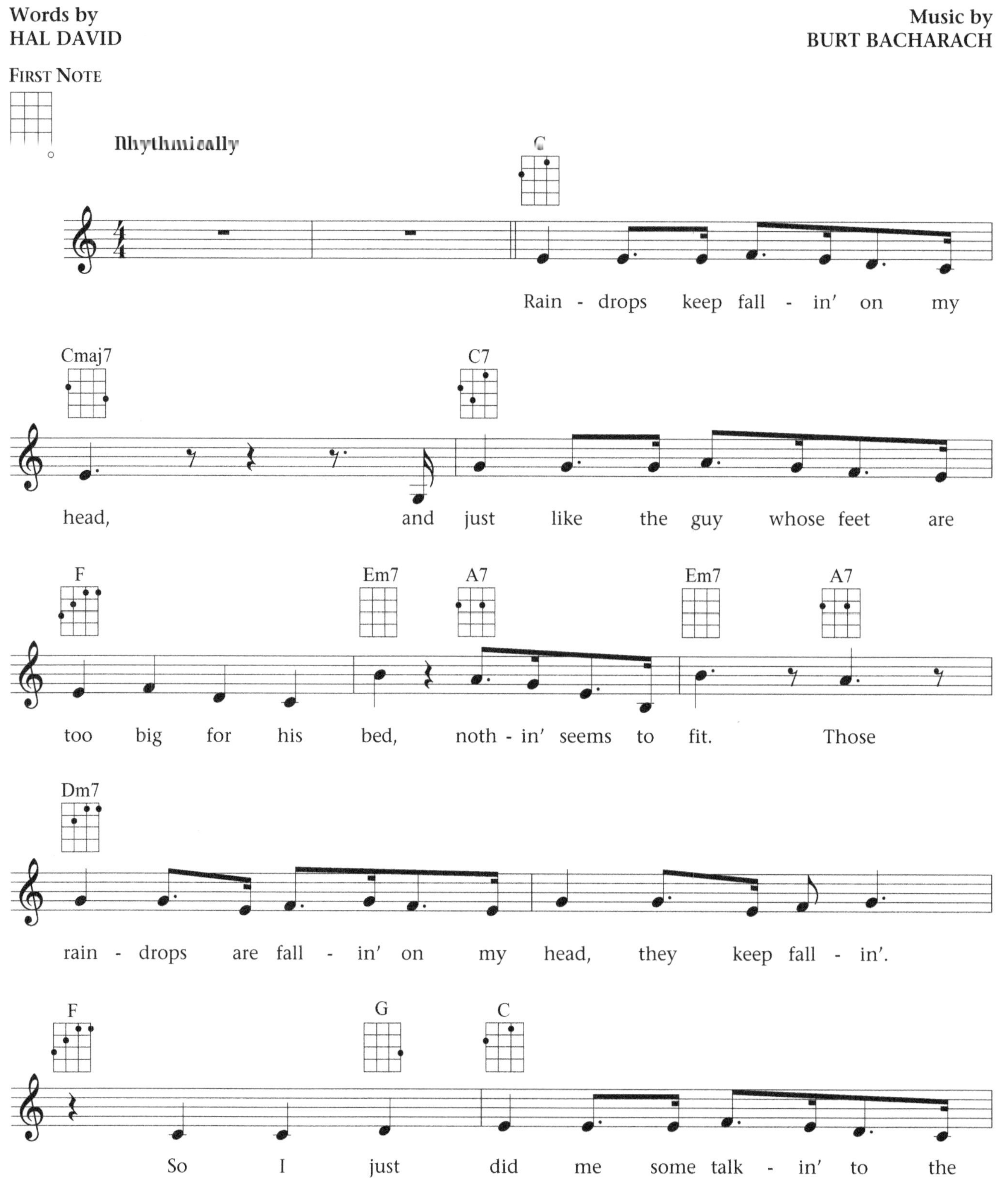

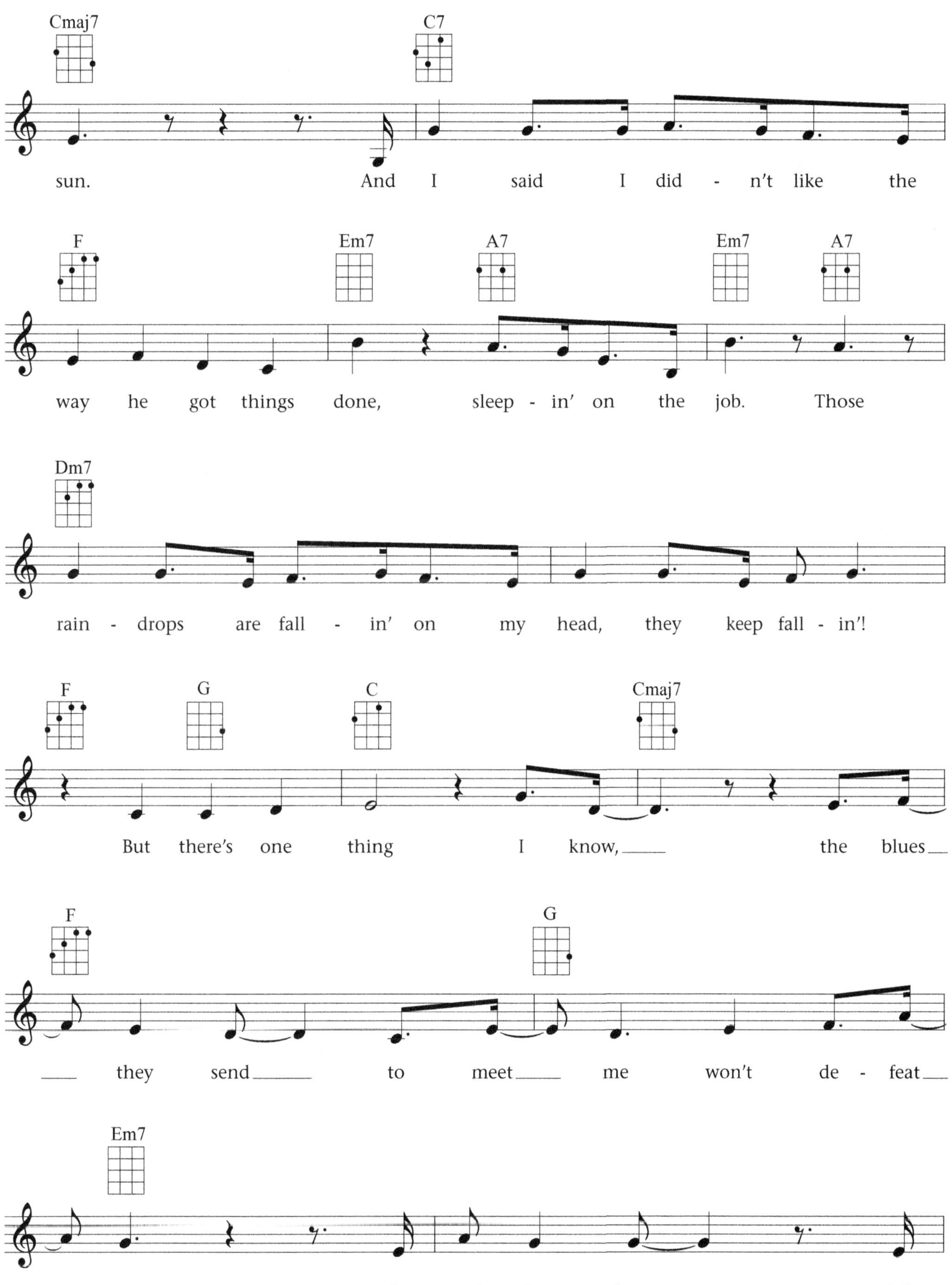
Cmaj7
C7
sun. And I said I did - n't like the
F
Em7
A7
Em7
A7
way he got things done, sleep - in' on the job. Those
Dm7
rain - drops are fall - in' on my head, they keep fall - in'!
F
G
C
Cmaj7
But there's one thing I know, the blues
F
G
they send to meet me won't de - feat
Em7
me. It won't be long 'til

A9
Dm7
hap - pi - ness steps up to greet me.
F
G
F
G
C
Rain - drops keep fall - in' on my
Cmaj7
C7
head, but that does - n't mean my eyes will
F
Em7
A7
Em7
A7
soon be turn - in' red. Cry - in's not for me, 'cause
Dm7
F
G
I'm nev - er gon - na stop the rain by com - plain - in'. Be - cause I'm
C
Cmaj7
Dm7
F
C
free, noth - in's wor - ry - in' me.

Red River Valley

Traditional

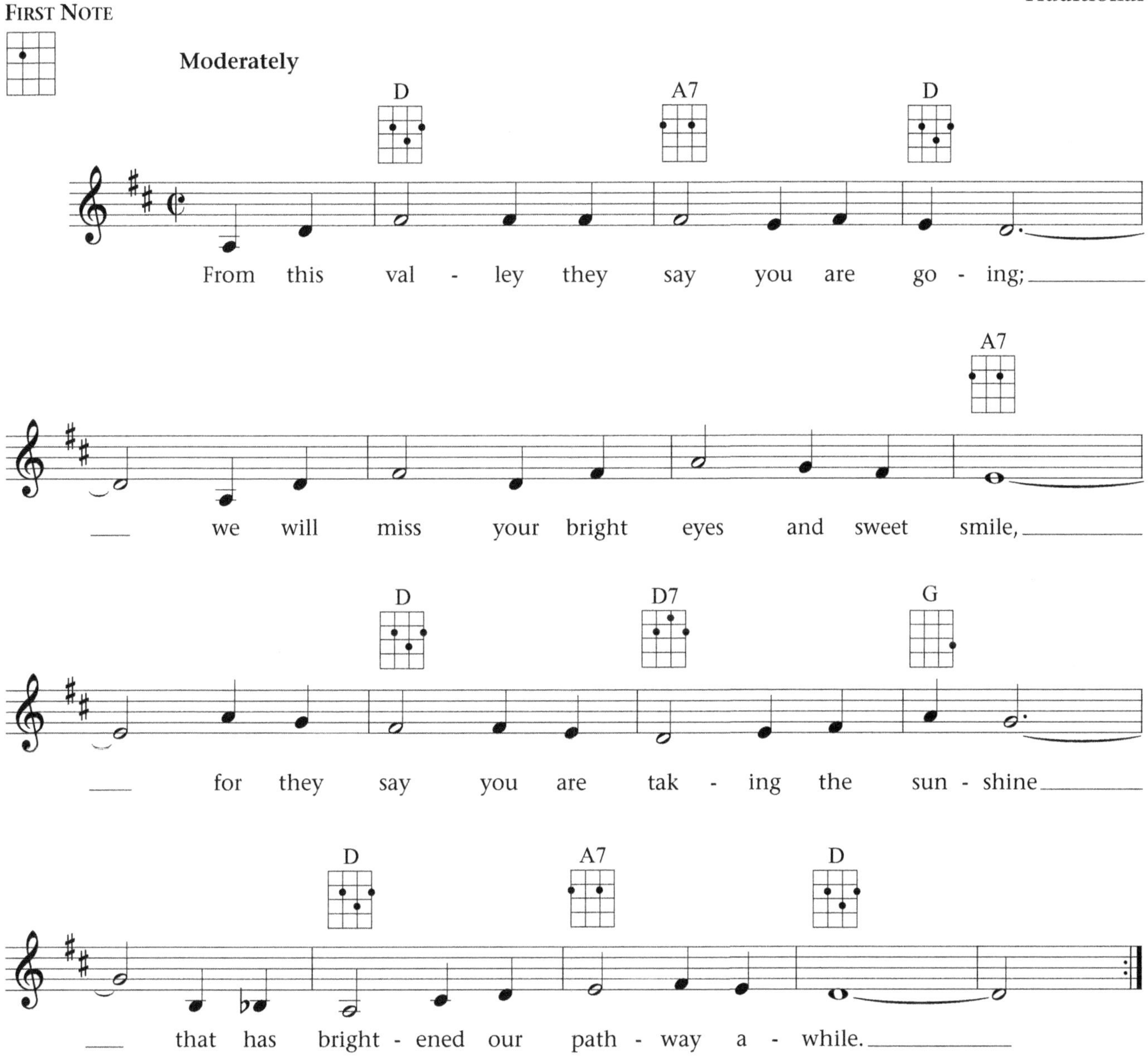

FIRST NOTE

Moderately

D A7 D

From this val - ley they say you are go - ing; ___

A7

___ we will miss your bright eyes and sweet smile, ___

D D7 G

___ for they say you are tak - ing the sun - shine ___

D A7 D

___ that has bright - ened our path - way a - while. ___

Additional Lyrics

2. Won't you think of this valley you're leaving?
Oh, how lonely, how sad it will be.
Oh, think of the fond heart you're breaking
and the grief you are causing me.

3. Come and sit by my side if you love me.
Do not hasten to bid me adieu,
but remember the Red River Valley
and the cowboy (cowgirl) that loves you so true.

Tennessee Waltz

Words and Music by
REDD STEWART and PEE WEE KING

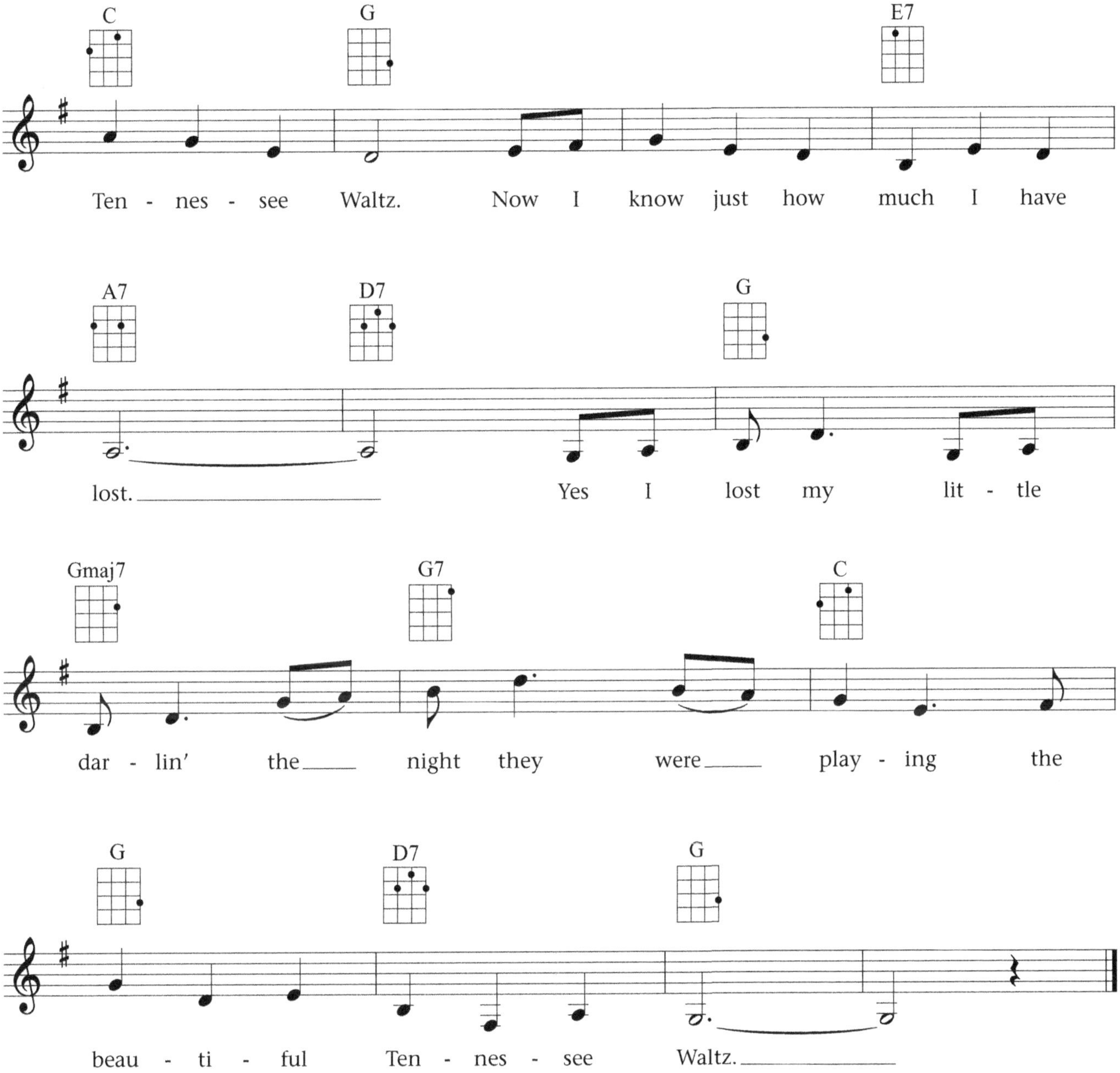
C G E7
Ten - nes - see Waltz. Now I know just how much I have
A7 D7 G
lost. Yes I lost my lit - tle
Gmaj7 G7 C
dar - lin' the night they were play - ing the
G D7 G
beau - ti - ful Ten - nes - see Waltz.

Smith's
SIMPLIFIED-ILLUSTRATED
BARITONE
UKULELE
METHOD and SONG FOLIO

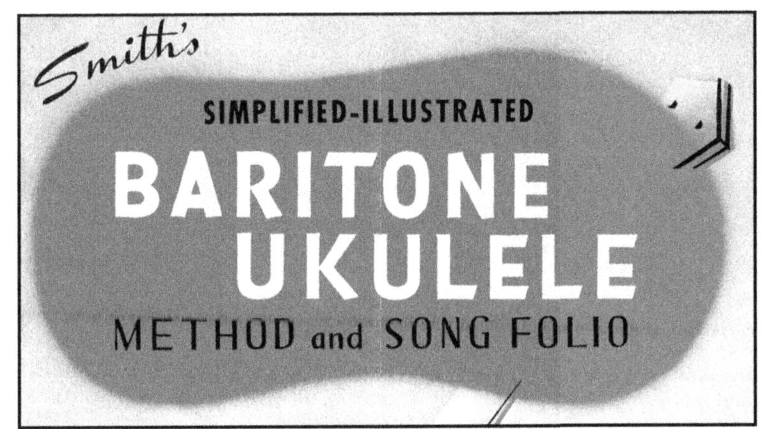

When I'm Sixty-Four

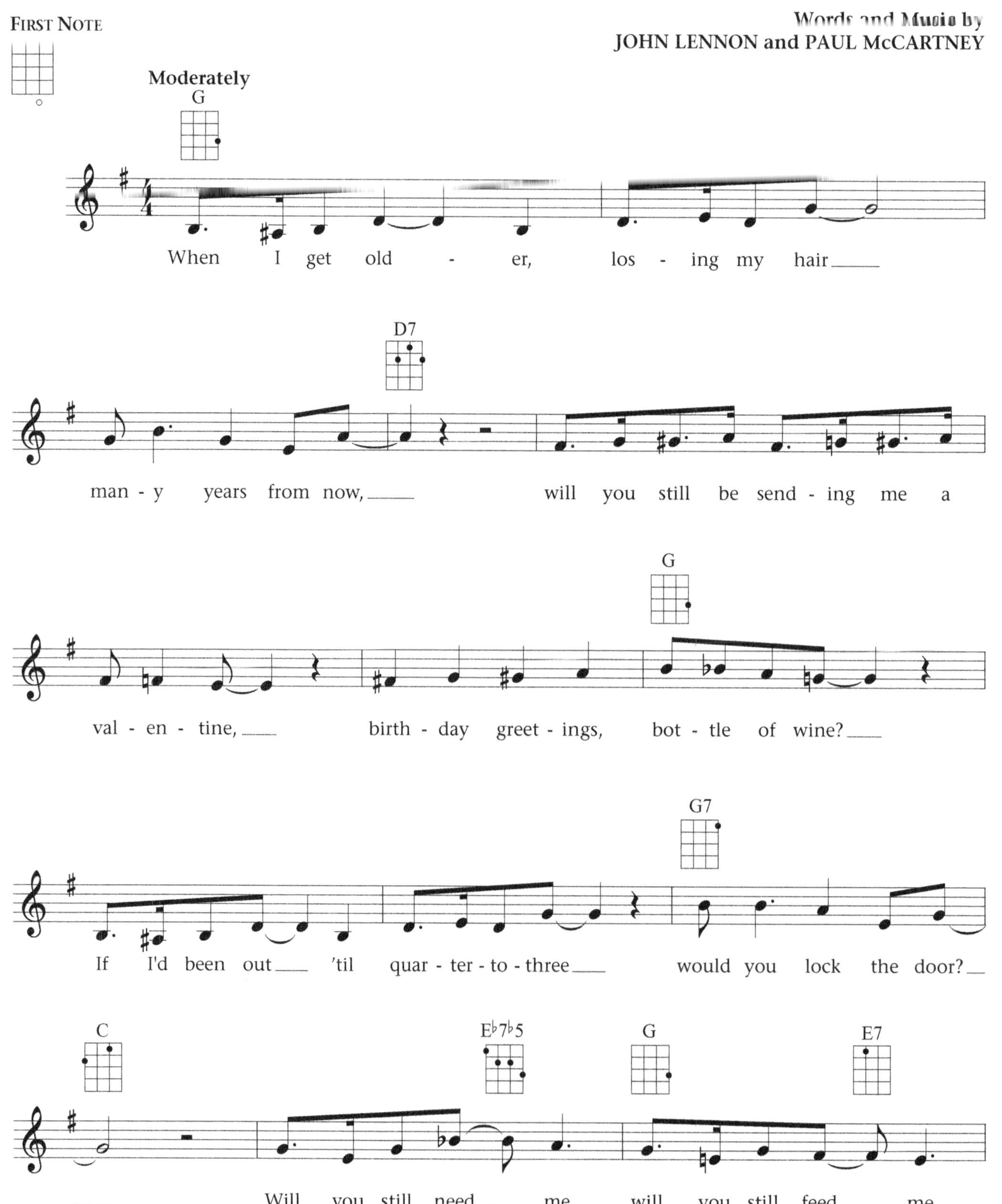

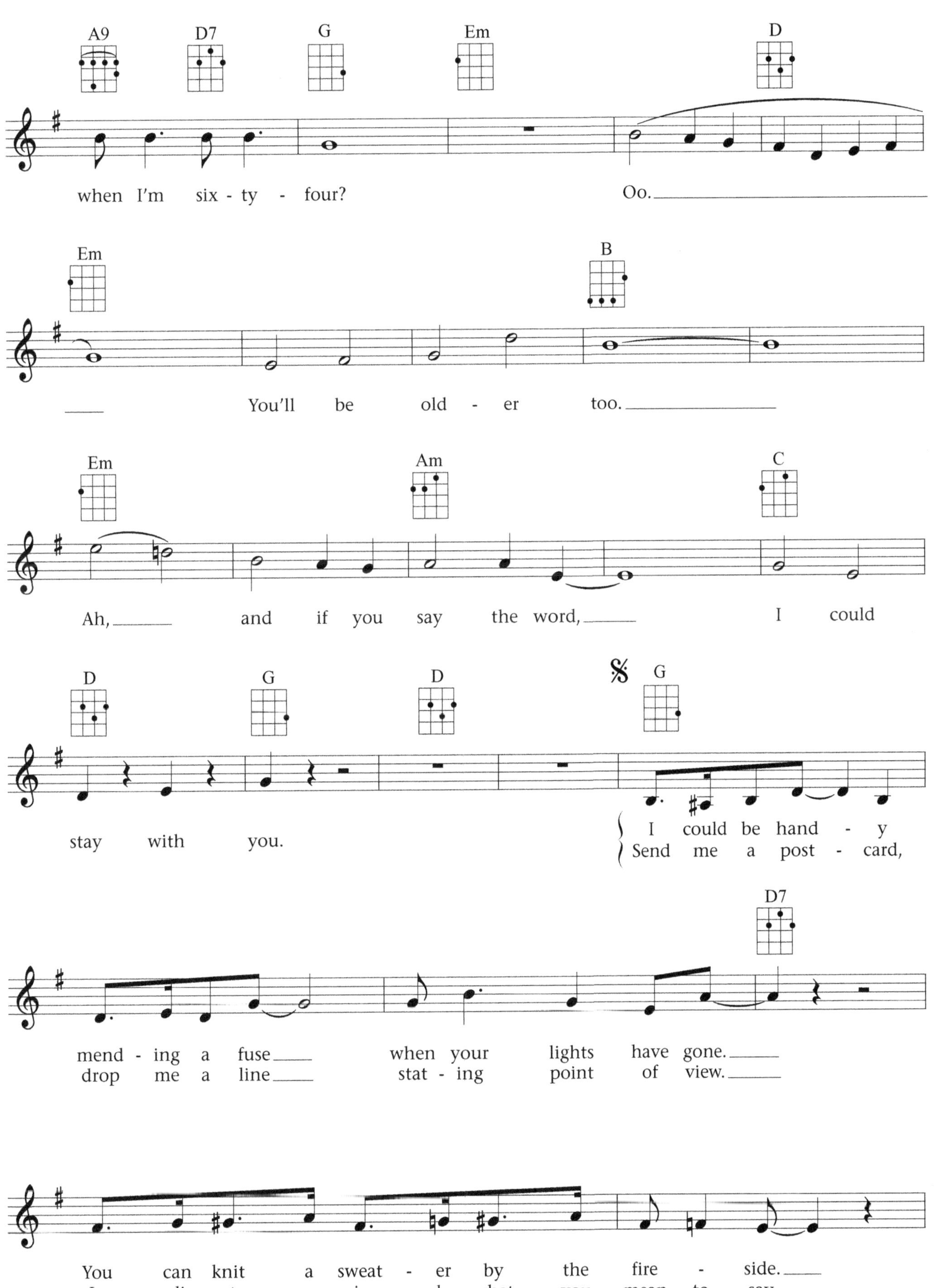
A9
D7
G
Em
D
when I'm six - ty - four?
Oo.
Em
B
You'll be old - er too.
Em
Am
C
Ah, and if you say the word, I could
D
G
D
G
stay with you.
I could be hand - y
Send me a post - card,
D7
mend - ing a fuse when your lights have gone.
drop me a line stat - ing point of view.
You can knit a sweat - er by the fire - side.
In - di - cate pre - cise - ly what you mean to say.

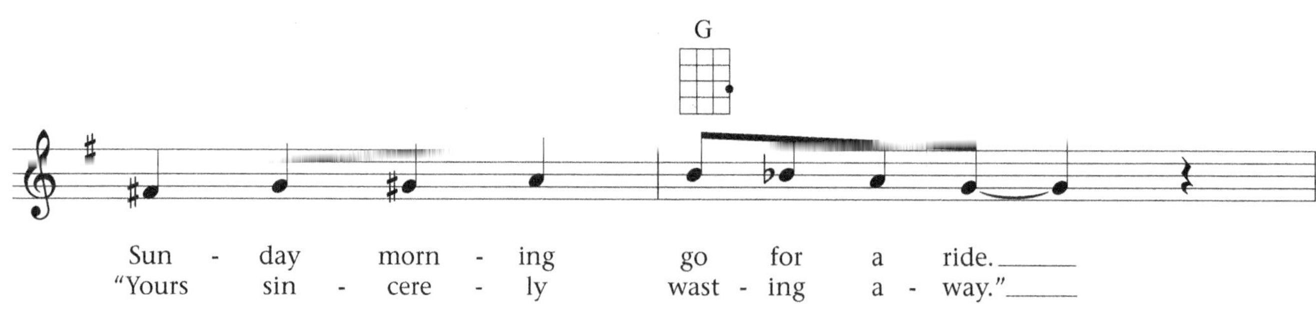

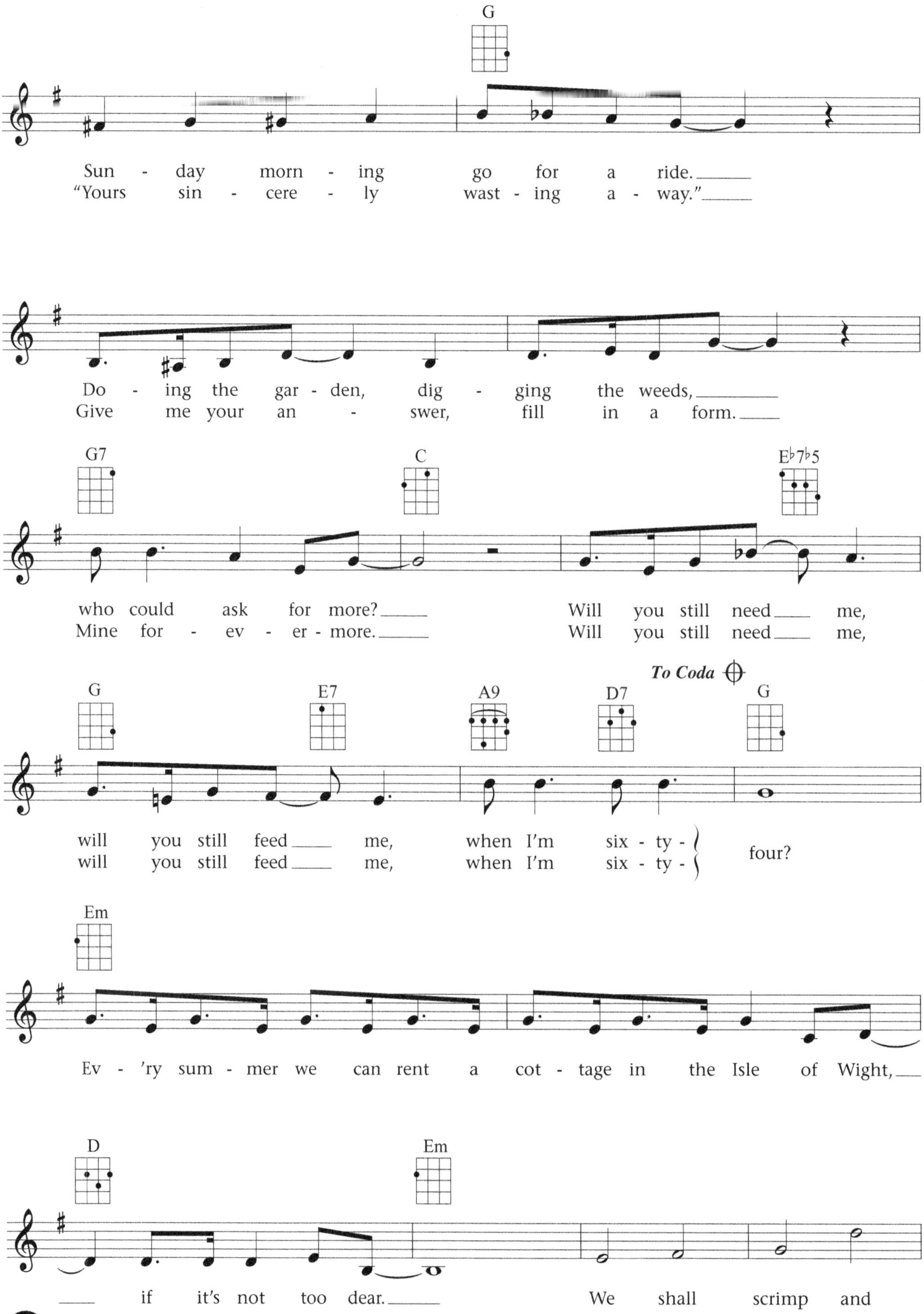

Do - ing the gar - den, dig - ging the weeds,
Give me your an - swer, fill in a form.

G7 C Eb7b5

who could ask for more?
Mine for - ev - er - more.
Will you still need me,
Will you still need me,

To Coda ⊕

G E7 A9 D7 G

will you still feed me, when I'm six - ty - four?
will you still feed me, when I'm six - ty - four?

Em

Ev - 'ry sum - mer we can rent a cot - tage in the Isle of Wight,

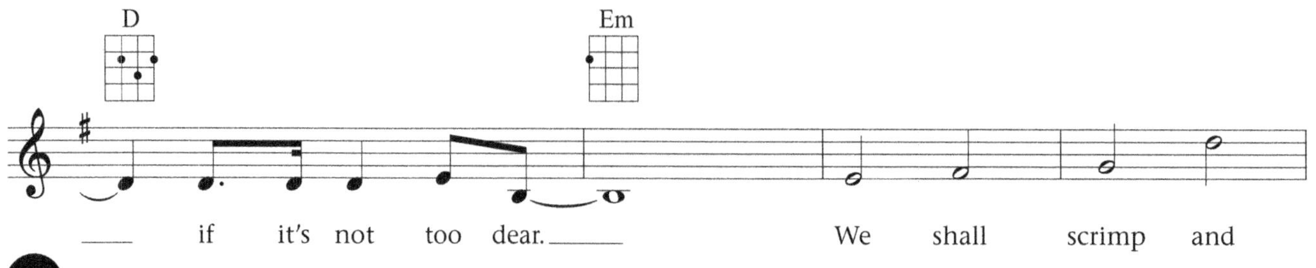

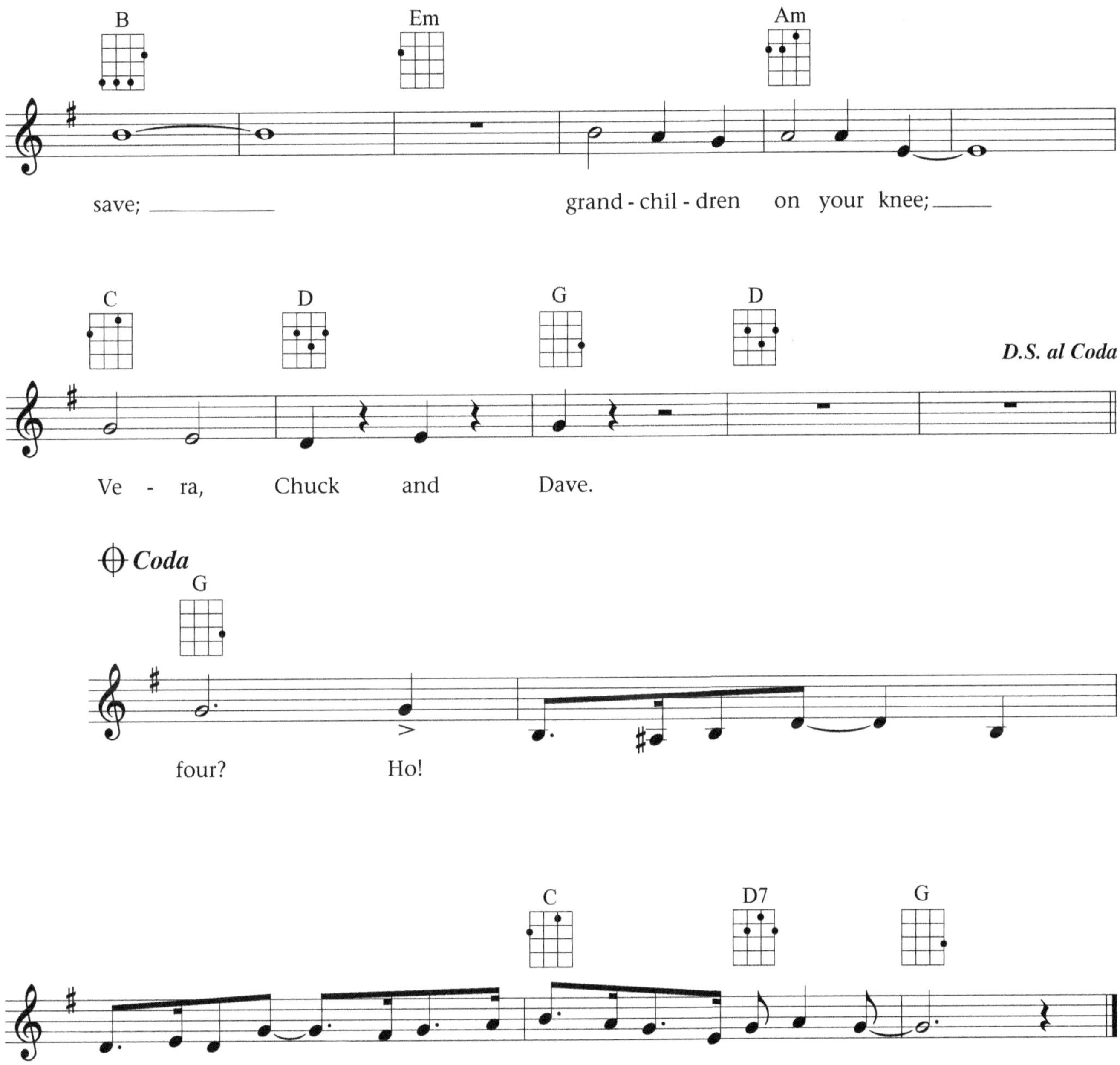

B Em Am

save; ______ grand - chil - dren on your knee; ______

C D G D *D.S. al Coda*

Ve - ra, Chuck and Dave.

Coda

G

four? Ho!

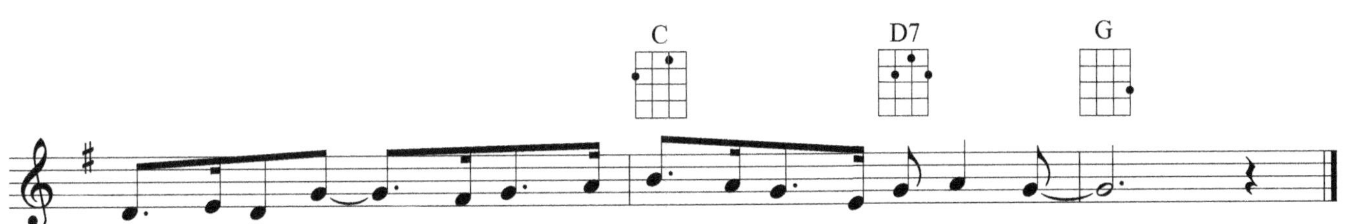

You Made Me Love You

Words by
JOE McCARTHY

Music by
JAMES V. MONACO

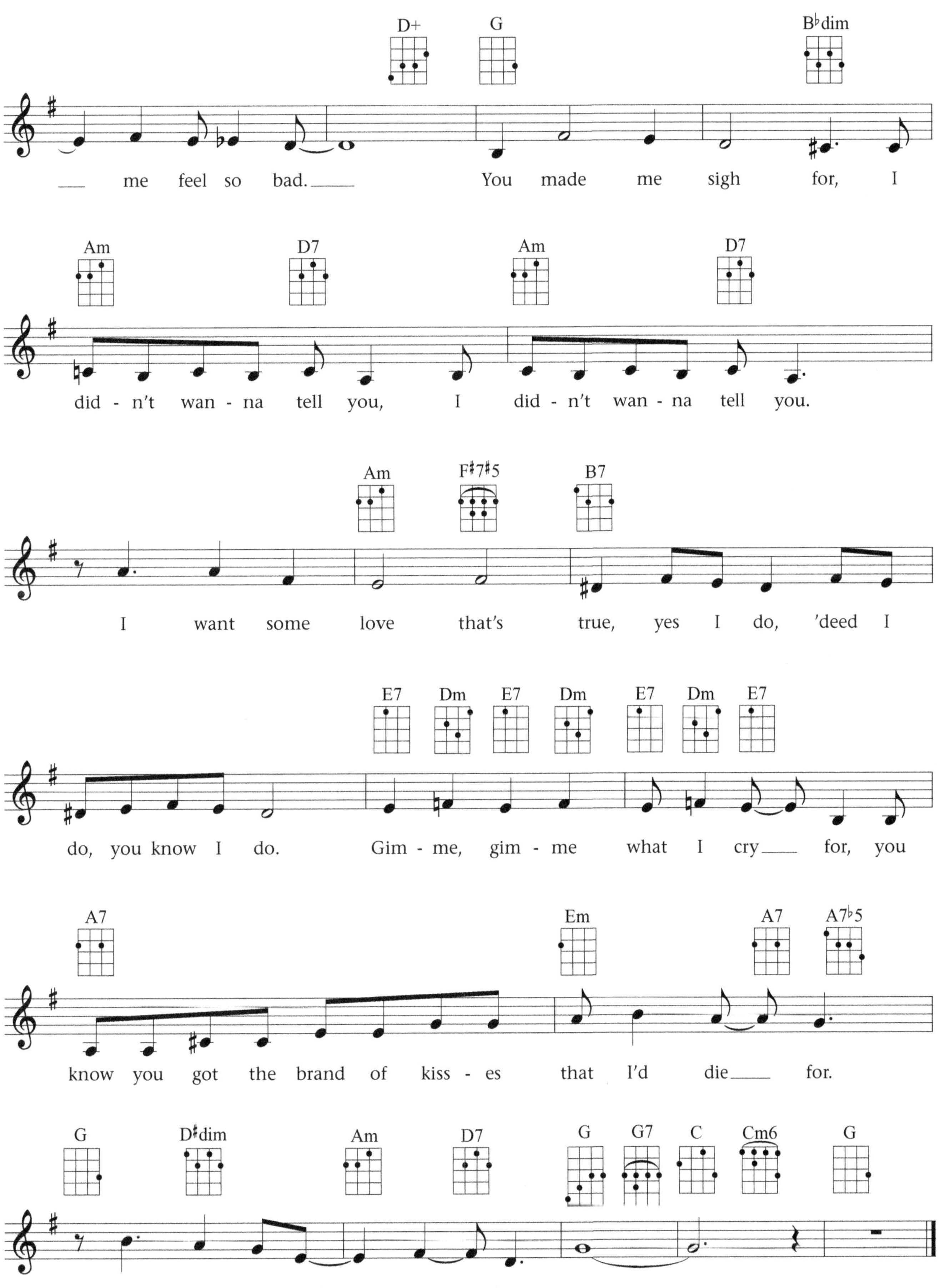
D+
G
B♭dim
__ me feel so bad. __ You made me sigh for, I
Am
D7
Am
D7
did - n't wan - na tell you, I did - n't wan - na tell you.
Am
F♯7♯5
B7
I want some love that's true, yes I do, 'deed I
E7
Dm
E7
Dm
E7
Dm
E7
do, you know I do. Gim - me, gim - me what I cry __ for, you
A7
Em
A7
A7♭5
know you got the brand of kiss - es that I'd die __ for.
G
D♯dim
Am
D7
G
G7
C
Cm6
G
You know you made __ me __ love you. ____

That Hawaiian Melody